T H E · B O O K · O F

Crepes & Omelets

T H E   B O O K   O F

Crepes & Omelets

MARY NORWAK

Photography by
JON STEWART

HPBooks

ANOTHER BEST SELLING VOLUME FROM HPBooks

Published by HPBooks, P.O. Box 5367, Tucson, AZ 85703   602/888-2150
1st Printing

©RPLA Pty Limited 1988

By arrangement with Salamander Books Ltd. and Merehurst Press, London.

Publisher: Rick Bailey
Executive Editor: Randy Summerlin
Editorial Director: Elaine R. Woodard
Editor: Jan Thiesen
Art Director: Don Burton
Book Design: Paul Fitzgerald
Managing Editor: Cindy J. Coatsworth
Typography: Beverly Fine
              Phyllis Hopkins
Director of Manufacturing: Anthony B. Narducci
Home Economist: Sarah Bush
Printed by New Interlitho S.p.A., Milan

Library of Congress Cataloging-in-Publication Data

Norwak, Mary.
  The book of crepes & omelets.

  Includes index.
  1. Pancakes, waffles, etc.   2. Omelets.
I. Title.   II. Title: Book of crêpes and omelets.
III. Title: Crêpes & omelets.
TX770.P34N67   1988   641.8   87-17602
ISBN 0-89586-669-2

CONTENTS

INTRODUCTION

Crepes and omelets are universal dishes. These simple egg mixtures are quickly prepared and fried to produce many delectable dishes, and nearly every country in the world has its own variations. Once the basic techniques are mastered, crepes and omelets can be served at every meal of the day, for fillings and flavorings can vary from the most simple to the very sophisticated.

The crepe is a mixture of flour, eggs and liquid cooked over high heat to a lacy fineness. Variations include thick puffy pancakes made from different grains. Each country has its own favorite toppings, ranging from caviar and sour cream to smoked fish, vegetables, meat and fruit, and a huge range of sweet tooth favorites. Crepes may be folded, rolled or formed into parcels, and coated in sauces—the variety is endless.

The omelet is an even more simple dish of eggs, butter and flavorings, but many people have not mastered the basic technique of preparation and serving. In this book, there are step-by-step instructions for the perfect golden omelet and its many savory and sweet variations. Here are the answers for producing the most delicious snacks as well as main courses and desserts which represent a triumph for the cook.

EQUIPMENT

A pan is the most important piece of equipment for making crepes and omelets. Other equipment needs are bowls and forks, which are in every kitchen.

Crepe and Omelet Pan

The pan may be made of cast iron or aluminum, or may be finished with a non-stick surface. It should be approximately 2 inches deep, with a thick base and curved sides. A 7-inch pan is most useful for crepes and 3-egg omelets; an 8- or 9-inch pan is best for 5- or 6-egg omelets.

The pan should be used exclusively for crepes and omelets, as it is important to keep the surface smooth so that the delicate mixtures do not stick.

Seasoning a Pan

All new pans, except the nonstick type, must be *seasoned* before use. Seasoning the pan refers to preparing a surface to which eggs will not stick, and which will remain smooth while cooking a batch of crepes or omelets. Old pans which tend to stick may also be seasoned. There are two good ways of doing this:

a) Cover the base of the pan with 1/2-inch of table salt. Place the pan over low heat and let it heat for 30 minutes until hot. Remove from heat and rub hard with a paper towels rolled into a ball. Set it aside until cool, then wipe with a dry cloth.

b) Cover the base of the pan with 1/2-inch olive oil. Heat very gently for 5 minutes. Remove from heat and let it stand for at least 12 hours. Pour off the oil

and wipe the surface of the pan with paper towels.

Care and Storage

A pan used for crepes and omelets should not be washed. After use, the pan should be wiped with paper towels and stored in a plastic bag. If you notice that ingredients begin to stick in the pan, do not wash but, instead, repeat the seasoning process.

Other Equipment

There are no specific requirements for other equipment needed to make crepes and omelets, and all the items are easily available.

A small saucepan may be needed for preparing fillings.

Scales may sometimes be necessary for weighing dry ingredients and fats.

A large bowl is useful for mixing so that plenty of air may be incorporated.

Measuring spoons—a tablespoon and a teaspoon—are needed for small quantities of ingredients.

A large fork or straight-edged rubber spatula is needed for omelet-making, to draw liquid egg from the sides to center of pan.

A flexible metal spatula is needed to turn crepes and to fold omelets, and to lift them onto serving dishes.

CREPE TECHNIQUES

The best crepes are thin, light and lacy, and indeed almost transparent. They may be served with a simple spread or other flavoring, or used as a "container" for substantial fillings. A similar batter mixture lightened by a rising agent such as baking powder or yeast may be cooked as small, thick, puffy pancakes to be served with a variety of toppings.

Ingredients

Batter for crepes is made with flour from wheat or other grains mixed with milk and eggs. A thin layer of this mixture is cooked in a heavy pan lightly greased with oil or butter. If a very light crisp crepe is desired, a little melted butter or flavorless oil may be added to the batter before cooking.

Basic Preparation

To prepare the crepe batter, sift flour and salt into a bowl. Make a well in the center and add eggs and a little milk. Beat with a wooden spoon, gradually incorporating flour from the edge of the bowl. As the mixture thickens, gradually add the milk. Beat well until smooth and then add remaining milk. Beat hard until bubbles form on top. Alternatively, this batter may also be prepared in a blender or food processor.

There is no need to let the batter stand before using. If left to stand, it will thicken, and a little more milk will probably be needed. The batter should be like thin cream to make light crepes.

Heat just enough oil in a crepe pan to cover the base. When a slight haze rises, pour in 2 to 3 tablespoons batter to cover base of pan thinly. Tilt the pan quickly so that the base is evenly covered with batter. Cook for about 1 minute until lightly browned underneath. Quickly turn the crepe with a metal spatula and cook the other side for 30 seconds. Lift out onto a warm plate, and continue cooking crepes until all the batter is used.

Fillings and Sauces

Crepes may be spread with jam, honey, fruit puree, or fruit juice and sugar. If the filling is slightly warmed, it will spread more easily without tearing the crepes. More substantial fillings are chopped fruit or ice cream for a dessert course. Savory fillings may be meat, fish, poultry, cheese or vegetables, mixed with sauce, yogurt or cream. Filled crepes may be covered in a cheese sauce and placed briefly under the broiler or in the oven to brown.

Storing and Reheating

Crepes are best when freshly cooked. To keep a batch warm for immediate use, place them in a stack in a warm oven, or on a plate over a pan of boiling water.

Crepes may be prepared in advance and stored in a refrigerator for 5 to 6 days. They should be stacked and wrapped in foil or a plastic bag. They may be quickly reheated by cooking in a lightly greased pan for 30 seconds on each side. Alternatively, the cold crepes may be wrapped around a filling and heated in the oven.

Freezing and Thawing

Stack cold crepes between pieces of parchment or waxed paper, and enclose in foil or a freezer bag. Freeze crepes for up to 6 months. To use the crepes, thaw at room temperature for 3 hours, or overnight in refrigerator. For speed, spread crepes individually and thaw at room temperature for 15 minutes. If preferred, remove parchment or waxed paper and stack 4 to 6 crepes together. Wrap in foil and heat in oven at 400F (205C) for 25 minutes.

FOLDING AND SERVING

Crepes may be served in many different ways. A 7-inch crepe is the most useful size for everyday eating. Here are some folding and serving suggestions for crepes:

  a) Serve flat with a topping arranged pizza-style on surface.

  b) Spread on a filling such as jam, or lemon juice and sugar, and fold twice to give a long flat roll.

  c) Spread filling on crepe and fold in half, then in half again to give triangular shape.

  d) Fold into quarters and open one "pocket" like a cone for filling.

  e) Place filling on crepe and fold in sides. Roll up lightly to make a rectangular parcel.

  f) Stack crepes like a cake with filling between each layer; cut into wedges to serve.

Basic Crepes

1 cup (4 oz.) all-purpose flour
Pinch of salt
2 eggs
1-1/4 cups milk
1 tablespoon butter, melted

Vegetable oil
Lemon juice and sugar *or* warmed jam

Sift flour and salt into a bowl. Make a well in the center and add the eggs and a little of the milk. Beat well with a wooden spoon, working in all the flour. Gradually beat in the remaining milk until bubbles form on top of batter. Stir in butter.

Add a small amount of oil to a 7-inch crepe pan—enough to barely cover the base—and place over high heat. Pour in 2 to 3 tablespoons batter and quickly tilt the pan so that the batter covers the base thinly and evenly. Cook for about 1 minute over high heat until lightly browned underneath.

Turn crepe with a metal spatula and cook other side for about 30 seconds. Keep crepe warm. Continue until batter is used. Serve with lemon juice and sugar, or with warmed jam. Makes 8 crepes.

Whole-Wheat Crepes

1 cup (4 oz.) whole-wheat flour
1/2 teaspoon salt
3 eggs
1-1/4 cups milk

Vegetable oil
Assorted toppings (pages 20-37)

Stir flour and salt in a bowl. Make a well in the center and add the eggs and a little of the milk. Beat well with a wooden spoon, working in all the flour. Gradually beat in the remaining milk until bubbles form on top of the batter.

Add a small amount of oil to a 7-inch crepe pan—enough to barely cover the base—and place over high heat. Pour in 2 to 3 tablespoons batter and quickly tilt the pan so that the batter covers the base thinly and evenly. Cook for about 1 minute over high heat until lightly browned underneath. Turn crepe with a metal spatula and cook other side for about 30 seconds. Keep crepe warm. Continue until batter is used. Serve with savory or sweet toppings. Makes 8 crepes.

———————— Buckwheat Crepes ————————

1-1/2 cups (6 oz.) buckwheat flour
1/2 cup (2 oz.) all-purpose flour
1/2 cup wheat germ
2 tablespoons brown sugar
2 teaspoons baking powder
Pinch of salt
2 eggs
2 tablespoons vegetable oil
About 1-1/4 cups milk or water

Vegetable oil
Smoked Salmon & Lemon Topping
  (page 24)
Parsley sprigs

Combine flours, wheat germ, brown sugar, baking powder and salt in a medium-size bowl; mix well. In another bowl, combine eggs and oil and mix well. Stir into the dry ingredients. Beat in enough milk or water to make a thick creamy batter.

Add a small amount of oil to a 7-inch crepe pan—enough to barely cover the base—and place over medium heat. Pour in 2 to 3 tablespoons batter and quickly tilt the pan so that the batter covers the base thinly and evenly. Cook gently until surface is set and covered with bubbles. Turn crepe with a metal spatula and cook other side until lightly browned. Keep crepe warm. Continue until batter is used. To serve, fold crepes into a cone shape and fill with topping. Garnish with parsley. Makes 8 crepes.

Oatmeal Crepes

1-2/3 cups (8 oz.) fine oatmeal
2 cups (8 oz.) all-purpose flour
Pinch of salt
1 (1/4-oz.) package active dry yeast
1 teaspoon sugar
1-1/4 cups lukewarm water

Vegetable oil
Seafood & Pepper Topping (page 20)

Combine oatmeal, flour and salt in a medium-size bowl. Add yeast, sugar and water and beat well. Cover and let stand in a warm area for 1 hour, until bubbly.

Add a small amount of oil to a 7-inch crepe pan—enough to barely cover the base—and place over medium heat. Pour in 2 to 3 tablespoons batter and quickly tilt the pan so that the batter covers the base thinly and evenly. Cook gently until surface is set and covered with bubbles. Turn crepe with a metal spatula and cook other side until lightly browned. Keep crepe warm. Continue until batter is used. To serve, stack crepes and spoon topping between each layer. Cut in wedges. Makes 8 crepes (4 servings).

Cornmeal Pancakes

1/2 cup (2 oz.) cornmeal
1-1/4 cups boiling water
1-1/4 cups milk
2 cups (8 oz.) all-purpose flour
2 tablespoons sugar
2 teaspoons baking powder
1 teaspoon salt
1 egg, beaten
2 tablespoons butter, melted

Vegetable oil
Butter and maple syrup

Pour the cornmeal into a small saucepan. Add water and simmer, stirring constantly, 5 minutes. Transfer to a medium-size bowl and beat in the milk. In another bowl, stir together flour, sugar, baking powder and salt. Beat into the cornmeal mixture. Beat in the egg and butter.

Place a heavy frying pan over high heat and grease lightly with oil. Pour in batter to make 3-inch rounds. Cook until surface is just set and covered with bubbles. Turn and cook other side until golden. Serve warm with butter and maple syrup. Makes 24 pancakes.

Blini

3 cups (12 oz.) buckwheat flour
2-1/2 cups milk
1 (1/4-oz.) package active dry yeast
3 eggs, separated
1/2 cup butter, room temperature
1/2 teaspoon salt

Vegetable oil
Caviar and sour cream, yogurt, *or*
  smoked or salted fish

Pour 1 cup flour into a warmed bowl. Heat 2/3 cup milk in a saucepan until lukewarm; stir in yeast. Beat into flour. Cover and let stand in a warm area 1 hour. In a large bowl, beat egg yolks with butter; gradually beat in the yeast mixture, remaining flour, milk and salt. Beat well until smooth. Let rise 30 minutes.

In a deep bowl, beat egg whites until stiff peaks form. Fold into batter. Heat a heavy skillet and grease lightly with oil. Pour in batter to make 3-inch rounds. Cook until surface is just set and covered with bubbles. Turn and cook other side until golden. Serve with caviar and sour cream, yogurt or fish. Makes about 15.

Puffy Yeast Pancakes

Sugar
2 cups (8 oz.) all-purpose flour
1 teaspoon sugar
**2/3 package (scant 2/3 tablespoon) active
dry yeast**
1-1/4 cups milk
1 egg, separated
1/2 teaspoon salt

Vegetable oil
**Raspberry Sauce Topping (page 29) or
other sweet topping (pages 28-37)**

Sprinkle waxed paper with sugar; set aside. Sift flour into a bowl. Stir in 1 teaspoon sugar and the yeast. Heat milk in a saucepan until lukewarm. Add to flour mixture and beat until smooth. Cover lightly and let stand in a warm area until batter is bubbly, stirring occasionally, about 30 minutes. Stir in egg yolk. In a small deep bowl, beat egg white with salt until stiff peaks form. Fold into batter.

Place a heavy skillet over medium-high heat and grease lightly with oil. Add batter by tablespoonfuls and cook until bottoms of pancakes are golden. Turn and cook second side. Transfer to sugared parchment. Serve hot with Raspberry Sauce Topping or other sweet topping. Makes 15 pancakes.

Potato Pancakes

2 large potatoes
1/2 cup (2 oz.) all-purpose flour
2 eggs
3/4 cup milk
Salt and pepper

Vegetable oil
Chicken, Bacon & Mushroom Topping
  (page 25) or other savory topping
  (pages 20-27)

Bring saucepan partially filled with salted
water to a boil. Peel potatoes. Add to
saucepan and boil 10 minutes. Drain well
and cool until easy to handle. Grate
coarsely into a bowl. Stir in flour. Beat
eggs and milk together until well mixed.
Gradually add to potatoes, beating with a
wooden spoon. Add salt and pepper.

Place a heavy skillet over medium-high
heat and grease lightly with oil. Add
about 1/4 cup potato mixture to make
pancakes about 1/4 inch thick. Cook until
golden on bottom, then turn and cook
other side. Keep pancakes warm. Continue until all batter is used. Serve hot with
topping. Makes 4 to 6 pancakes.

Seafood & Pepper Topping

Oatmeal Crepes (page 15) or other crepes
  or pancakes (pages 12-19)

2 tablespoons butter
1 small red pepper, finely chopped
1/4 cup all-purpose flour
1-1/4 cups milk
1/2 cup (2 oz.) shredded Cheddar cheese
8 oz. smoked cod or haddock fillets,
  cooked and flaked
4 oz. (about 1 cup) peeled and deveined
  cooked shrimp
1/2 teaspoon dry mustard
Lemon slices and parsley sprigs

Keep crepes warm while preparing topping. Melt butter in a medium-size skillet
over low heat. Add red pepper and cook
until pepper is just soft. Add flour and
cook, stirring constantly, 1 minute. Remove from heat and gradually stir in milk.
Bring to a boil and stir until thickened.

Stir in cheese, cod, shrimp and mustard.
Stir over low heat until warmed through.
Serve over crepes or pancakes. Garnish
with lemon and parsley. Serves 4.

Egg & Tomato Topping

**Basic Crepes (page 12) or other crepes or
  pancakes (pages 12-19)**

**1 tablespoon butter
1 medium-size onion, chopped
1 (14-oz.) can tomatoes
Salt and pepper
1/2 teaspoon sugar
1 tablespoon Worcestershire sauce
6 hard-cooked eggs, chopped
Watercress sprigs**

Keep crepes warm while preparing topping. Heat butter in a medium-size saucepan over low heat. Add onion and cook until soft, about 5 minutes. Add tomatoes, salt, pepper, sugar and Worcestershire. Simmer uncovered, stirring occasionally, 10 minutes.

Add eggs and simmer, stirring constantly, 2 minutes. Serve over crepes or pancakes. Garnish with sprigs of watercress. Serves 4.

Mexican Topping

**Basic Crepes (page 12) or other crepes or
pancakes (pages 12-19)**

**1/2 lb. ground beef
1 celery stalk, finely chopped
1 medium-size onion, finely chopped
1 (14-oz.) can tomatoes
1 (7-oz.) can corn, drained
2 tablespoons tomato puree
2 teaspoons chili powder or to taste
Celery leaves**

Keep crepes warm while preparing topping. Combine beef, celery and onion in a
medium-size saucepan. Cook over medium heat, stirring frequently, 5 minutes.
Drain off excess fat.

Stir in tomatoes, corn, tomato puree and
chili powder. Simmer, stirring occasionally, 10 minutes. Serve over crepes or
pancakes. Garnish with celery leaves.
Serves 4.

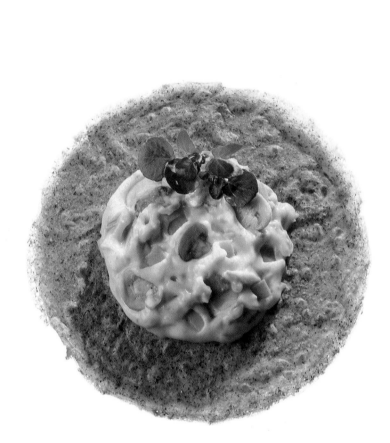

——Ham, Cheese & Mushroom Topping——

**Basic Crepes (page 12) or other crepes or
pancakes (pages 12-19)**

Cheese Sauce:
**2 tablespoons butter
1/4 cup all-purpose flour
1-1/4 cups milk
1 cup (4 oz.) shredded Cheddar cheese
Salt and pepper**

**2 tablespoons butter
4 oz. (about 1/2 cup) mushrooms, thinly
sliced
1/2 lb. cooked lean ham, finely chopped
Watercress sprigs**

Keep crepes warm while preparing topping. *For sauce:* Melt 2 tablespoons butter in a small saucepan over low heat. Stir
in flour and cook 1 minute. Remove from
heat and gradually stir in milk. Bring to a
boil and stir constantly until thickened.
Remove from heat and stir in cheese, salt
and pepper. Set aside.

Melt remaining butter in a small skillet
over low heat. Add mushrooms and cook,
stirring frequently, 3 minutes. Stir in ham
and cook 1 minute. Reheat cheese sauce
gently and stir in mushroom and ham
mixture. Serve over crepes or pancakes.
Garnish with watercress. Serves 4.

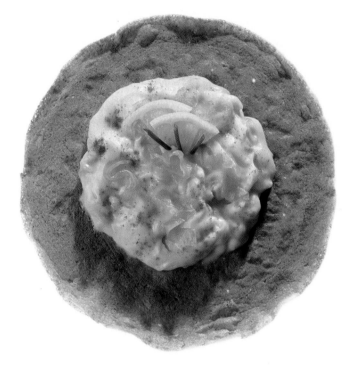

—— Smoked Salmon & Lemon Topping ——

**Basic Crepes (page 12) or other crepes or
  pancakes (pages 12-19)**

Lemon Sauce:
2 tablespoons butter
1/4 cup all-purpose flour
1-1/4 cups milk
3 tablespoons lemon juice
2 egg yolks, beaten
Salt and pepper

4 oz. smoked salmon, cut in thin strips
Ground red pepper
Lemon slices and chopped fresh chives

Keep crepes warm while preparing topping. *For sauce:* Melt butter in a small saucepan over low heat. Stir in flour and cook, stirring constantly, 1 minute. Remove from heat and gradually stir in milk. Bring to a boil and stir constantly until thickened. Stir in lemon juice. Remove from heat and stir in egg yolks. Season with salt and pepper.

Sprinkle salmon lightly with red pepper. Stir gently into the sauce. Serve over crepes or pancakes. Garnish with lemon slices and chives. Serves 4.

— Chicken, Bacon & Mushroom Topping —

**Basic Crepes (page 12) or other crepes or
  pancakes (pages 12-19)**

**1/4 lb. lean bacon, diced
2 tablespoons butter
1/2 lb. button mushrooms, thinly sliced
1 cup diced cooked chicken
2/3 cup half and half
Salt and pepper
Mint leaves**

Keep crepes warm while preparing topping. Cook bacon in a medium-size skillet over low heat until crisp and the fat is
rendered; drain lightly. Add butter and
mushrooms and cook, stirring frequently,
5 minutes. Stir in chicken and heat
through.

Remove from heat and stir in half and half
until ingredients are well coated. Return
to low heat just long enough to warm
through. Season with salt and pepper. To
serve, fold crepes or pancakes into a cone
shape and fill with topping. Garnish with
mint leaves. Serves 4.

Sausage & Bacon Topping

**Basic Crepes (page 12) or other crepes or
pancakes (pages 12-19)**

8 pork link sausages (about 1/2 lb.)
4 lean slices bacon, coarsely chopped
**4 oz. (about 1/2 cup) button mushrooms,
finely sliced**
1 teaspoon chopped fresh chives
**Additional whole and chopped fresh
chives to garnish**

Keep crepes warm while preparing topping. Broil or fry sausages until golden-
brown. Cut each sausage into about 4
pieces; set aside. Cook bacon in a
medium-size skillet over low heat until
bacon is crisp and the fat is rendered. Stir
in mushrooms and cook, stirring frequently, 3 minutes. Stir in sausage and
chives and heat through. To serve, fold
crepes or pancakes into a cone shape and
fill with topping. Garnish with extra
chives. Serves 4.

Bacon & Pineapple Topping

Basic Crepes (page 12) or other crepes or pancakes (pages 12-19)

1/2 lb. sliced bacon, coarsely chopped
8 canned pineapple rings, drained
Watercress sprigs

Keep crepes warm while preparing topping. Heat large skillet over medium-low heat. Add bacon and cook until crisp and the fat is rendered.

Cut each pineapple ring in eighths. Add to bacon and cook just long enough to heat through. To serve, fold crepes or pancakes into a cone shape and fill with topping. Garnish with sprigs of watercress. Serves 4.

Honeyed Banana Topping

**Basic Crepes (page 12) or other crepes or
pancakes (pages 12-19)**

**3 medium-size bananas
2 teaspoons lemon juice
1/4 cup light honey
Pinch of nutmeg (preferably freshly
grated)**

Keep crepes warm while preparing topping. Peel bananas; slice in strips into a
medium-size bowl. Add lemon juice and
toss gently but thoroughly to coat banana.

Warm honey in a 1-quart saucepan over
low heat. Add bananas and heat until just
warm. Season with nutmeg. Spoon over
crepes or pancakes. Serves 4.

Raspberry Sauce Topping

**Basic Crepes (page 12) or other crepes or
pancakes (pages 12-19)**

**1 (10- to 12-oz.) pkg. frozen raspberries
in syrup, thawed
2/3 cup water
2 tablespoons sugar
1 tablespoon cornstarch
2 tablespoons cold water
Raspberry leaves to decorate**

Keep crepes warm while preparing topping. Drain raspberry syrup into a small saucepan. Add 2/3 cup water and the sugar and bring to a boil over medium heat. Meanwhile, combine cornstarch with cold water in a small bowl; mix well. Stir in boiling liquid. Return to saucepan and bring to boil over low heat, stirring frequently, until sauce thickens.

Remove from heat and stir in raspberries. Heat gently, being careful not to break up fruit. Spoon over crepes or pancakes and decorate with raspberry leaves. Serves 4.

Honey-Orange Topping

**Basic Crepes (page 12) or other crepes or
pancakes (pages 12-19)**

2 oranges
3 tablespoons lemon juice
1/4 cup light honey
Toasted coconut and strips of orange zest

Keep crepes warm while preparing topping. Peel oranges, removing all white pith. Using a sharp knife, and holding the orange over a bowl to collect the juice, cut between the membranes and release orange segments.

Combine orange juice, lemon juice and honey in a small saucepan. Place over low heat and warm gently 3 minutes. Add orange segments and stir 2 minutes. Spoon over crepes or pancakes. Garnish with coconut and orange strips. Serves 4.

Apricot & Lemon Topping

Basic Crepes (page 12) or other crepes or
   pancakes (pages 12-19)

1/2 cup (2 oz.) dried apricots, chopped
   and soaked overnight in 1-1/4 cups
   water
5 tablespoons apricot jam
2 tablespoons lemon juice
1 teaspoon grated lemon or lime zest
   (colored part only)
Slivers of lemon or lime zest

Keep crepes warm while preparing topping. Drain apricots, reserving liquid.
Combine apricots with 6 tablespoons of
the liquid in a small saucepan. Place over
low heat and let simmer 5 minutes.

Add jam, lemon juice and grated zest and
cook, stirring constantly, 5 minutes.
Spoon over crepes or pancakes. Garnish
with slivered zest. Serves 4.

Banana Cream Topping

**Basic Crepes (page 12) or other crepes or
  pancakes (pages 12-19)**

2/3 cup whipping cream
2 large bananas
2 tablespoons powdered sugar
2 teaspoons lemon juice
1/2 teaspoon grated nutmeg
Pecan halves, if desired

Keep crepes warm while preparing topping. In a medium-size bowl, beat cream until soft peaks form. Peel bananas; mash them in another medium-size bowl with sugar and lemon juice. Fold the cream into the bananas. Season with nutmeg. To serve, fold crepes or pancakes into a cone shape and arrange on serving plates. Mound topping in center and garnish with pecans. Serves 4.

Rich Butterscotch Topping

**Basic Crepes (page 12) or other crepes or
 pancakes (pages 12-19)**

3/4 cup packed brown sugar
2 tablespoons all-purpose flour
1/2 cup butter, softened
1/2 cup milk
Toasted slivered almonds

Keep crepes warm while preparing topping. Combine sugar, flour and butter in a
small saucepan and beat with a wooden
spoon until well mixed. Place over low
heat and stir occasionally until butter
melts and mixture comes to a boil. Boil 3
minutes, stirring constantly.

Remove from heat and gradually add
milk. Return to heat and beat until smooth
and mixture boils again. Spoon over
crepes or pancakes and garnish with
almonds. Serves 4.

Orange Liqueur Topping

**Basic Crepes (page 12) or other crepes or
pancakes (pages 12-19)**

**1 medium-size orange
1/4 cup butter, softened
3/4 cup powdered sugar
2 tablespoons orange-flavored liqueur
Orange slices and slivered zest**

Make crepes ahead and keep warm, or
make crepes while topping chills. Grate
zest (colored part only) from orange;
transfer to a 1-cup glass measure.
Squeeze orange juice and add to zest; set
aside. In another small bowl, cream butter and sugar until light and fluffy.

Gradually add zest and orange juice to
butter mixture and beat well. Gradually
add orange liqueur and beat until soft and
creamy. Chill for 30 minutes before serving. Pipe or spoon over crepes or pancakes and garnish with orange slices and
slivered zest. Serves 4.

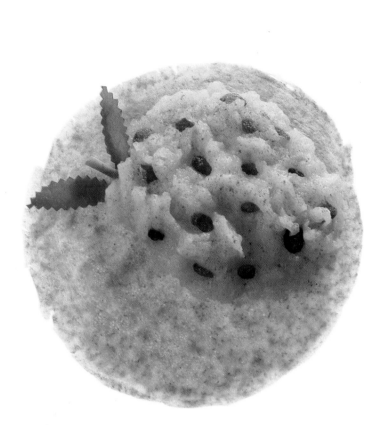

Apple & Raisin Topping

**Basic Crepes (page 12) or other crepes or
pancakes (pages 12-19)**

1 lb. red-skinned cooking apples
2/3 cup water
1/3 cup sugar
1/3 cup raisins
2 teaspoons lemon juice
1/4 teaspoon ground cinnamon
A few slivers of lime zest

Keep crepes warm while preparing topping. Peel and core apples, reserving
some larger pieces of peel for garnish, if
desired; slice apples thinly. Place in small
saucepan and add water and sugar. Cook
over low heat until apples are soft. Meanwhile, with pinking shears cut reserved
apple peel in leaf shapes; place in bowl of
cold water.

Puree apples in food processor or blender,
or press through a sieve. Return to pan
and simmer until thick, about 5 minutes.
Stir in raisins, lemon juice and cinnamon.
Simmer 1 minute. Spoon over crepes or
pancakes. Garnish with apple "leaves"
and slivered lime "stems." Serves 4.

Fresh Lemon Topping

**Basic Crepes (page 12) or other crepes or
pancakes (pages 12-19)**

2 lemons
1-1/4 cups water
1/4 cup sugar
2 tablespoons cornstarch
**2 tablespoons lemon curd (purchased or
homemade)**

Keep crepes warm while preparing topping. Grate zest (colored part only) from
lemons; transfer to small saucepan.
Squeeze juice from lemons and add to
pan. Reserve 3 tablespoons water; add
remaining water and sugar to pan. Place
over low heat and cook, stirring occasionally, until sugar is melted.

In a small bowl, combine reserved water
with cornstarch. Stir in a small amount of
the hot liquid and mix well. Return to pan
and add lemon curd. Stir over low heat
until sauce is thick and clear. Serve over
crepes or pancakes. Garnish with thin
strips of lemon zest, if desired. Serves 4.

Jamaican Banana Topping

**Basic Crepes (page 12) or other crepes or
pancakes (pages 12-19)**

1/2 cup butter
3/4 cup packed brown sugar
1 lemon
3 medium-size bananas
2 tablespoons dark rum
**Lemon twists and thin strips of lemon
zest, if desired**

Keep crepes warm while preparing topping. Combine butter and sugar in a small
saucepan. Place over low heat and stir
until butter is melted. Grate zest (colored
part only) from lemon; squeeze juice from
lemon. Stir zest and juice into saucepan
and simmer, stirring, 1 minute.

Peel bananas; slice thinly. Stir into saucepan and cook gently 2 minutes. Remove
from heat and stir in rum. Serve over
crepes or pancakes. Garnish with lemon
twists and lemon zest. Serves 4.

Gruyère & Anchovy Crepes

7-inch crepes (page 12, 13, 14 or 15)

1 (3-oz.) can anchovies, drained
4 oz. Gruyère, Samsø or Tybo cheese, cut
  in small, thin strips
2/3 cup sour cream
1 tablespoon lemon juice
Salt and pepper
Chopped fresh parsley and additional
  shredded cheese

Keep crepes warm while preparing filling. Reserve 4 anchovy fillets for garnish; chop the rest finely. In a small bowl, combine anchovies, cheese, sour cream and lemon juice. Season with salt and pepper.

Divide filling between crepes. Roll up and place on serving plates. Garnish with reserved anchovy fillets, parsley and cheese. Serve at once. Serves 4.

Mozzarella & Crouton Crepes

7-inch crepes (page 12, 13, 14 or 15)

1/4 cup butter
1 (1-inch) thick slice bread, cubed
1 cup (4 oz.) diced Mozzarella cheese
Salt and pepper
1/3 cup grated Parmesan cheese
Basil sprigs

Keep crepes warm while preparing filling. Heat butter in a small skillet over medium heat. Add bread cubes and cook, stirring often, until golden. Remove from heat and stir in Mozzarella. Season with salt and pepper.

Preheat broiler. Divide filling between crepes. Roll up and arrange in a single layer in a shallow heatproof dish. Sprinkle with Parmesan. Broil until lightly browned, about 2 minutes. Garnish with sprigs of basil. Serves 4.

Italian Ricotta Crepes

7-inch crepes (page 12, 13, 14 or 15)

1 cup ricotta cheese
1 tablespoon grated Parmesan cheese
1 tablespoon chopped fresh marjoram
Salt and pepper
2 tablespoons butter
2 teaspoons all-purpose flour
2 tablespoons tomato puree
2/3 cup chicken broth
Marjoram sprigs to garnish

Keep crepes warm while preparing filling. In a medium-size bowl, combine ricotta, Parmesan, marjoram, salt and pepper and beat until creamy. Divide filling between crepes. Fold in quarters and arrange in single layer in shallow heatproof dish.

Preheat broiler. Melt butter in a small saucepan. Stir in flour. Cook, stirring, 30 seconds. Stir in tomato puree, broth, salt and pepper and simmer 3 minutes. Spoon over crepes. Broil until lightly browned, about 2 minutes. Garnish with sprigs of marjoram. Serves 4.

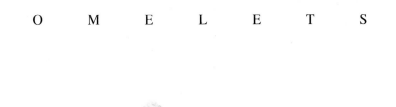

Parmesan Crepes

7-inch crepes (page 12, 13, 14 or 15)

2 tablespoons vegetable oil
2 tablespoons butter
1/2 lb. potatoes, cooked and diced
Salt and pepper
1 cup fresh bread crumbs
1/4 cup butter, melted
1 tablespoon chopped fresh parsley
2/3 cup grated Parmesan cheese
Parsley sprigs

Keep crepes warm while preparing filling. Heat oil and 2 tablespoons butter in a medium-size skillet over medium-high heat. Add potatoes and cook until crisp and golden; drain well. Season with salt and pepper.

Preheat broiler. Spoon potatoes in center of crepes. Roll up and arrange in a single layer in a shallow heatproof dish. In a small bowl, combine bread crumbs, melted butter and chopped parsley; sprinkle over crepes. Top with Parmesan. Broil about 6 inches from heat source until crisp and golden, 4 to 5 minutes. Garnish with sprigs of parsley. Serves 4.

Asparagus Crepes

7-inch crepes (page 12, 13, 14 or 15)

12 fresh or canned asparagus tips, plus additional asparagus tips for garnish, if desired
2 tablespoons butter
2 teaspoons all-purpose flour
2/3 cup half and half
1 teaspoon chopped fresh parsley
1 teaspoon chopped fresh chives
Salt and pepper
1 tablespoon grated Parmesan cheese

Keep crepes warm while preparing filling. If asparagus is fresh, cook in boiling salted water until crisp-tender, about 6 minutes; drain well. If asparagus is canned, drain well. Melt butter in a small saucepan over low heat. Stir in flour and cook 30 seconds. Stir in half and half and cook, stirring frequently, until thick. Stir in parsley, chives, salt and pepper.

Preheat broiler. Set aside any asparagus being used for garnish; stir remaining asparagus into sauce. Divide filling between crepes. Roll up and arrange in a single layer in a shallow heatproof dish. Top with reserved asparagus and sprinkle with Parmesan. Broil until cheese is melted and lightly browned, about 2 minutes. Serves 4.

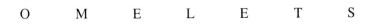

Crepes with Corn-Cheese Sauce

7-inch crepes (page 12, 13, 14 or 15)

1 medium-size onion, finely chopped
2 tablespoons butter
1 (14-oz.) can corn, drained
Cheese Sauce (page 23)
1 teaspoon chopped fresh marjoram
1/4 cup (1 oz.) shredded Cheddar cheese
Marjoram sprigs

Keep crepes warm while preparing filling. In a medium-size saucepan, combine onion and butter. Cook over low heat until onion is softened, about 5 minutes. Stir in corn and heat through. Reserve 6 tablespoons Cheese Sauce; add remaining sauce and the chopped marjoram to pan.

Preheat broiler. Place one crepe on a large heatproof plate. Spread with some of the corn mixture. Top with a second crepe. Repeat until all crepes are used, finishing with a crepe on top. Top with reserved Cheese Sauce and sprinkle with Cheddar. Broil until sauce is bubbling, about 3 minutes. To serve, cut in wedges. Garnish with marjoram sprigs. Serves 4.

Neapolitan Crepes

7-inch crepes (page 12, 13, 14 or 15)

2 tablespoons butter
1 tablespoon olive oil
1 lb. onions, thinly sliced
1 (14-oz.) can tomatoes
1 (3-oz.) can anchovies, drained and
  chopped
3 tablespoons tomato puree
8 pimiento-stuffed olives, sliced
1 teaspoon chopped fresh basil
Salt and pepper
4 pimiento-stuffed olives, halved
Basil leaves

Keep crepes warm while preparing filling. Combine butter and oil in a medium-size saucepan over low heat. Add onions and cook 5 minutes. Add undrained tomatoes, anchovies, tomato puree, sliced olives, basil, salt and pepper. Cover and simmer 30 minutes, stirring occasionally.

Preheat oven to 350F (175C). Divide filling between crepes. Roll up and arrange in single layer in shallow heatproof dish. Cover with foil. Bake 20 minutes. Garnish with olives and basil. Serves 4.

Mushroom Crepes

7-inch crepes (page 12, 13, 14 or 15)

1/4 cup butter
1/2 lb. mushrooms, thinly sliced
1/2 cup all-purpose flour
1-1/4 cups milk
1/4 teaspoon grated nutmeg
Salt and pepper
Chopped parsley and parsley sprigs

Keep crepes warm while preparing filling. Melt butter in a medium-size saucepan over low heat. Add all but 4 mushroom slices; cover and cook 5 minutes. Stir in flour and cook 1 minute. Gradually stir in milk. Bring to a boil, stirring constantly, then simmer 3 minutes. Season with nutmeg, salt and pepper.

Preheat oven to 350F (175C). Divide filling between crepes. Roll up and arrange in a single layer in a shallow heatproof dish. Cover with foil. Bake 20 minutes. Garnish with reserved mushroom slices and parsley. Serves 4.

Spinach Crepes

7-inch crepes (page 12, 13, 14 or 15)

2 lbs. fresh spinach, well-washed

2 tablespoons butter
1 medium-size onion, finely chopped
1 tablespoon tomato puree
1 teaspoon paprika
2 hard-cooked eggs, chopped
Salt and pepper
1/3 cup grated Parmesan cheese
Parsley sprigs

Keep crepes warm while preparing filling. Wash spinach thoroughly. Place in a large pan, using only water that clings to leaves. Cover and cook over low heat until spinach is tender and limp. Drain well, then press out as much moisture as possible. Chop spinach finely; set aside.

Melt butter in a medium-size saucepan over low heat. Add onion and cook until soft, about 5 minutes. Stir in tomato puree and paprika and simmer 2 minutes. Stir in eggs. Season with salt and pepper. Preheat broiler. Divide spinach between crepes and spread evenly. Top with egg mixture. Roll up and arrange in a single layer in a shallow heatproof dish. Sprinkle with Parmesan. Broil until lightly browned, about 2 minutes. Garnish with parsley sprigs. Serves 4.

— Smoked Trout & Cream Cheese Crepes —

4 green onions for garnish, if desired

7-inch crepes (page 12, 13, 14 or 15)

6 oz. smoked trout, flaked
3 green onions, finely chopped
1/2 (8-oz.) pkg. cream cheese, room
temperature
2 tablespoons half and half
1 teaspoon lemon juice
Salt and pepper

Make garnish by cutting ends of green onions to form "flowers"; place in bowl of ice water to allow flowers to "bloom." Make crepes; keep warm while preparing filling. In a small bowl, combine trout, green onions, cream cheese and half and half and beat until soft and well mixed. Add lemon juice, salt and pepper.

Preheat oven to 300F (150C). Divide mixture between crepes. Roll up and arrange in a single layer in a shallow heat-proof dish. Bake 15 minutes. Garnish with green onion flowers. Serves 4.

Salmon Supreme Crepes

7-inch crepes (page 12, 13, 14 or 15)

2 tablespoons butter
1 medium-size onion, finely chopped
2 oz. button mushrooms, thinly sliced
2 tablespoons all-purpose flour
2/3 cup half and half
1 (7-oz.) can red salmon, drained and
　flaked
3/4 cup cooked peas
1/2 cup (2 oz.) shredded Gruyère, Samsø
　or Tybo cheese
1 teaspoon lemon juice
Salt and pepper
1/3 cup grated Parmesan cheese
Lemon twists and parsley sprigs.

Keep crepes warm while preparing filling. Melt butter in a medium-size saucepan over low heat. Add onion and mushrooms and cook until soft, about 5 minutes. Stir in flour and cook 1 minute. Remove from heat and stir in half and half. Return to low heat and cook, stirring, until thick and smooth; do not allow sauce to boil. Remove from heat and stir in salmon, peas, cheese, lemon juice, salt and pepper.

Preheat oven to 350F (175C). Divide filling between crepes. Roll up and arrange in a single layer in a shallow heatproof dish. Sprinkle with Parmesan. Bake 25 minutes. Garnish with lemon twists and sprigs of parsley. Serves 4.

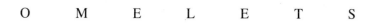

Fish Crespolini

7-inch crepes (page 12, 13, 14 or 15)

3/4 lb. white fish fillets
2 cups milk
2 tablespoons butter
2 tablespoons all-purpose flour
4 medium-size tomatoes, peeled, seeded
    and chopped
1 tablespoon lemon juice
Salt and pepper
3/4 cup (3 oz.) shredded Cheddar cheese
Watercress sprigs and sliced cherry
    tomatoes

Keep crepes warm while preparing filling. Arrange fish in a medium-size skillet; cover with half the milk. Poach until fish is just cooked through. Remove fish with slotted spoon; reserve poaching liquid. Flake fish and set aside. Melt butter in a small saucepan over low heat. Stir in flour and cook 30 seconds. Remove from heat and stir in reserved liquid and remaining milk. Return to low heat and cook, stirring constantly, until sauce is thick and smooth. Divide sauce in half.

Preheat oven to 375F (190C). Stir fish, tomatoes and lemon juice into half the sauce; season with salt and pepper. Divide between crepes. Roll up and arrange in single layer in shallow heatproof dish. Stir cheese into remaining sauce and spoon over crepes. Bake until sauce is bubbling, about 20 minutes. Garnish with watercress and tomatoes. Serves 4.

Shrimp & Tuna Crepes

7-inch crepes (page 12, 13, 14 or 15)

3 tablespoons butter
1 small green pepper, finely chopped
1 tablespoon all-purpose flour
2/3 cup chicken broth
4 oz. (about 1 cup) peeled and deveined cooked shrimp
1 (7-oz.) can water-packed tuna, drained, flaked
2/3 cup half and half
Salt and pepper
Lemon slices and tarragon sprigs

Keep crepes warm while preparing filling. Melt butter in a medium-size saucepan over low heat. Add green pepper and cook just until softened. Add flour and cook 1 minute, stirring well. Stir in chicken broth and simmer, stirring constantly, until thick. Mix in shrimp and tuna. Stir in half and half and heat through but do not boil. Season with salt and pepper.

Preheat oven to 350F (175C). Divide mixture between crepes. Roll up and arrange in a single layer in shallow heatproof dish. Cover with foil. Bake 15 minutes. Garnish with lemon slices and tarragon sprigs. Serves 4.

—————— Smoked Fish & Egg Crepes ——————

7-inch crepes (page 12, 13, 14 or 15)

8 oz. smoked cod or haddock fillets
1-1/4 cups milk
2 tablespoons butter
2 tablespoons all-purpose flour
1 tablespoon lemon juice
2 hard-cooked eggs, chopped
2 teaspoons chopped fresh dill
1/3 cup grated Parmesan cheese
Lemon slices and sprigs of dill to garnish

Keep crepes warm while preparing filling. Arrange fish in a medium-size skillet; cover with milk. Poach until fish is just cooked through. Remove fish with slotted spoon; reserve poaching liquid. Flake fish and set aside. Melt butter in a small saucepan over low heat. Stir in flour and cook 30 seconds. Remove from heat and stir in reserved liquid. Return to heat and stir constantly until thick and smooth.

Remove from heat and stir in fish, lemon juice, eggs and dill. Preheat broiler. Divide mixture between crepes. Roll up and arrange in single layer in shallow heat-proof dish. Sprinkle with Parmesan. Broil until lightly browned, about 2 minutes. Garnish with lemon slices and sprigs of dill. Serves 4.

Savory Beef Crepes

7-inch crepes (page 12, 13, 14 or 15)

Cheese Sauce (page 23)

1 tablespoon butter
1 medium-size onion, finely chopped
3/4 lb. ground beef
2/3 cup beef broth
2 tablespoons tomato puree
Pinch of dried thyme
Salt and pepper
1 tablespoon grated Parmesan cheese

Prepare the crepes and Cheese Sauce and keep warm while preparing meat filling. Melt butter in a medium-size skillet over low heat. Add onion and cook until soft, about 5 minutes. Stir in meat and cook, stirring frequently, 5 minutes. Add broth, tomato puree, thyme, salt and pepper. Cover and simmer 15 minutes.

Preheat broiler. Divide meat mixture between crepes. Roll up and arrange close together in a single layer in a heatproof dish. Spoon Cheese Sauce over the top; sprinkle with Parmesan. Broil until golden-brown and bubbling, 2 to 3 minutes. Serves 4.

Curried Chicken Crepes

7-inch crepes (page 12, 13, 14 or 15)

1 medium-size onion, finely chopped
1 tablespoon butter
2 teaspoons curry powder
2 tablespoons all-purpose flour
1-1/4 cups chicken broth
3/4 lb. cooked chicken, diced
1 tablespoon lemon juice
Salt and pepper

Keep crepes warm while preparing filling. Combine onion and butter in a medium-size saucepan. Cook over low heat until onion is soft, about 5 minutes. Stir in curry powder and cook 30 seconds. Stir in flour and cook 30 seconds. Gradually add broth and bring to a boil, stirring constantly.

Stir in chicken and lemon juice. Season with salt and pepper. Cook over low heat, stirring constantly, 10 minutes. Divide mixture between crepes. Roll up and serve immediately. Garnish with slices of green pepper and lemon and sprigs of mint, if desired. Serves 4.

———————— Bolognese Crepes ————————

7-inch crepes (page 12, 13, 14 or 15)

2 tablespoons butter
1 small garlic clove, crushed
1 large onion, finely chopped
1 lb. ground beef
2 tablespoons all-purpose flour
1 (14-oz.) can tomatoes
2 teaspoons tomato puree
Salt and pepper
1/3 cup grated Parmesan cheese
Sprigs of watercress and tomato halves to
   garnish

Keep crepes warm while preparing filling. Melt butter in a medium-size skillet over low heat. Add garlic and onion and cook until onion is soft, about 5 minutes. Add ground beef and cook, stirring to break up meat, 5 minutes. Stir in flour and cook 1 minute. Stir in undrained tomatoes and puree. Simmer until thickened, about 10 minutes. Season with salt and pepper.

Preheat broiler. Place one crepe on a large heatproof plate. Spread with some of the filling. Top with a second crepe. Repeat until all crepes are used, finishing with a crepe on top. Sprinkle with Parmesan. Broil until lightly browned, about 2 minutes. To serve, cut in wedges. Garnish with watercress and tomatoes. Serves 4.

Sweet & Sour Pork Crepes

7-inch crepes (page 12, 13, 14 or 15)

1/2 lb. boneless pork shoulder, cubed
Vegetable oil
8 oz. can pineapple tidbits in syrup
1 tablespoon red currant jelly
1 tablespoon brown sugar
1 tablespoon vinegar
1 tablespoon cornstarch
2/3 cup tomato juice
Salt and pepper
Bean sprouts and green onion flowers
(page 47)

Keep crepes warm while preparing filling. Heat oil in a medium-size saucepan over low heat. Add pork and cook until tender and cooked through, about 10 minutes. Drain pineapple juice into small saucepan. Add jelly, brown sugar, vinegar and cornstarch and mix well. Add tomato juice and bring to a boil, stirring constantly. Reduce heat and simmer, stirring occasionally, until sauce is thick. Stir in pork and pineapple. Season with salt and pepper.

Preheat oven to 375F (190C). Divide pork mixture between crepes. Roll up and arrange in single layer in shallow heatproof dish. Cover with foil. Bake 20 minutes. Garnish with bean sprouts and green onion flowers. Serve immediately. Serves 4.

Caribbean Crepes

7-inch crepes (page 12, 13, 14 or 15)

4 medium-size bananas
2 teaspoons lemon juice
2/3 cup whipping cream
2 tablespoons brown sugar
Grated nutmeg

Keep crepes warm while preparing filling. Peel bananas. Thinly slice one banana; sprinkle with lemon juice and set aside. In a medium-size bowl, whip cream until stiff; set aside about 1/4 for decoration.

Mash remaining bananas in a medium-size bowl. Fold into 3/4 whipped cream along with sugar and 1/2 teaspoon nutmeg. To serve, cut each crepe in half and fold into a cone shape. Fill with whipped cream mixture. Decorate with rosettes of reserved whipped cream and banana slices; sprinkle banana slices with additional nutmeg. Serves 4.

Apricot Meringue Crepes

7-inch crepes (page 12, 13, 14 or 15)

6 tablespoons apricot jam
1 tablespoon lemon juice
2 egg whites
1/2 cup sugar
8 glacé cherries, whole or halved, and
candied angelica, if desired

Keep crepes warm while preparing filling. Combine jam and lemon juice in a small saucepan and heat gently, stirring frequently, until well mixed. Place one crepe on a large heatproof plate. Spread with a thin layer of warm jam. Cover with second crepe. Repeat until all the crepes are used.

Preheat oven to 450F (230C). In a medium-size bowl, beat egg whites until stiff peaks form; gradually beat in sugar. Lightly spread this meringue over the top crepe. Decorate with cherries and angelica. Bake until meringue is pale golden, about 2 minutes. Cut in wedges and serve immediately. Serves 4.

—— Cherry & Almond Layered Crepes ——

7-inch crepes (page 12, 13, 14 or 15)

1 (14-oz.) can cherries
6 tablespoons cherry jam
1 tablespoon lemon juice
1/2 cup ground almonds
2 eating pears, peeled and thinly sliced
1 tablespoon powdered sugar, sifted

Keep crepes warm while preparing filling. Drain cherries, reserving juice. Measure jam into a medium-size saucepan. Place over low heat and warm just until syrupy. Stir in 2 tablespoons reserved cherry juice, the lemon juice, almonds and pears. Remove from heat and stir in cherries.

Preheat oven to 325F (165C). Place one crepe on a large heatproof plate. Spread with some of the filling. Top with a second crepe. Repeat until all the crepes are used. Bake 10 minutes. Sprinkle with powdered sugar. Cut into wedges and serve immediately. Serves 4.

Blackberry & Apple Stack

7-inch crepes (page 12, 13, 14 or 15)

1 lb. cooking apples
12 oz. blackberries
1/2 cup sugar
2 egg whites

Keep crepes warm while preparing filling. Peel and core apples; chop coarsely. In a medium-size saucepan, combine apples, blackberries and 1/4 cup sugar. Place over low heat and simmer until fruit is soft. Let stand 10 minutes to cool. Place one crepe on a heatproof plate. Spread with some of filling. Top with a second crepe. Repeat until all the crepes are used, finishing with a crepe on top.

Preheat oven to 325F (165C). In a medium-size bowl, beat egg whites until stiff; gradually beat in remaining sugar. Cover top and sides of crepes with this meringue. Bake until golden brown, about 15 minutes. Cut in wedges and serve immediately. Serves 4.

─────── French Chestnut Crepes ───────

7-inch crepes (page 12, 13, 14 or 15)

1 (8-oz.) can sweetened chestnut puree
6 tablespoons orange juice
1 tablespoon lemon juice
1 tablespoon rum
2 tablespoons butter, melted
1 tablespoon powdered sugar

Preheat oven to 300F (150C). Spread each crepe with chestnut puree. Fold into quarters and arrange in shallow heatproof dish. In a small bowl, combine orange juice, lemon juice and rum. Pour over crepes. Cover loosely with foil. Bake 30 minutes. Remove from oven and discard foil.

Preheat broiler. Brush crepes with butter and sprinkle with powdered sugar. Broil until glazed, about 2 minutes. Serve immediately. Serves 4.

Crepes Suzette

7-inch crepes (page 12, 13, 14 or 15)

1/3 cup unsalted butter
1/2 cup powdered sugar
3 tablespoons orange juice
1 tablespoon lemon juice
2 tablespoons orange-flavored liqueur

1 tablespoon brandy
Orange slices and bay leaves

Fold each crepe in quarters. Combine butter, sugar, orange juice and lemon juice in a large skillet. Heat gently until mixture is syrupy. Stir in liqueur.

Add crepes and turn each once to coat with sauce. Pour on brandy and light quickly with a match. Arrange on plates and garnish with orange slices and bay leaves. Serve immediately. Serves 4.

—— Lemon Meringue Layered Crepes ——

7-inch crepes (page 12, 13, 14 or 15)

Fresh Lemon Topping (page 36)

2 egg whites
1/4 cup sugar
2 oz. (1/2 cup) slivered almonds, toasted
Candied angelica

Keep crepes warm while preparing Fresh Lemon Topping. Place one crepe on a heatproof plate. Spread with some of topping. Cover with a second crepe. Repeat until all the crepes are used, finishing with a crepe on top.

Preheat oven to 425F (220C). In a medium-size bowl, beat egg whites until stiff; gradually beat in sugar. Cover top and sides of crepes with this meringue. Top with almonds. Bake until pale golden, about 2 minutes. Decorate with angelica. Cut in wedges and serve immediately. Serves 4.

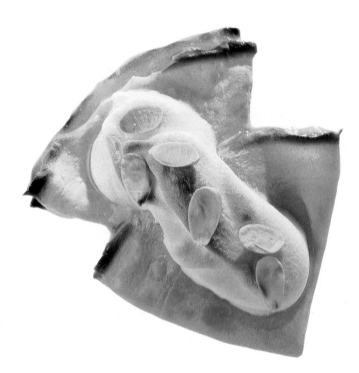

Apricot Delight

7-inch crepes (page 12, 13, 14 or 15)

**12 oz. (3 cups) dried apricots, chopped
and soaked overnight**
1/3 cup sugar
1 lemon
2 egg whites
1/4 cup sugar
1 tablespoon slivered almonds

Keep crepes warm while preparing filling. In a medium-size saucepan, combine apricots with just enough water to cover. Add sugar. Simmer, stirring occasionally, until fruit is soft. Puree in food processor or blender. Grate zest (colored part only) from lemon; squeeze lemon juice. Add zest and juice to the apricot puree.

Preheat oven to 375F (190C). Spoon a little of the puree on each crepe. Fold crepes in quarters and arrange in a single layer in a shallow heatproof dish. Cover with foil. Bake 30 minutes. In a medium-size bowl, beat egg whites until stiff; gradually beat in sugar. Remove crepes from oven and discard foil. Preheat broiler. Spoon meringue over crepes; sprinkle with almonds. Broil until lightly browned, about 2 minutes. Serves 4.

Orange Liqueur Gâteau

7-inch crepes (page 12, 13, 14 or 15)

1 (8-oz.) can mandarin oranges
2 teaspoons cornstarch
1 tablespoon light honey
1 tablespoon apricot jam
3 tablespoons orange-flavored liqueur
3 kiwifruit, sliced
2/3 cup whipping cream

Keep crepes warm while preparing filling. Drain oranges well, reserving juice; set oranges aside. Mix cornstarch with 1 tablespoon juice. In a small saucepan, combine remaining juice with honey and jam. Bring to boil over low heat. Add cornstarch mixture and stir until thick and clear. Stir in 2 tablespoons liqueur.

Place one crepe on a heatproof plate. Arrange a few mandarin oranges and kiwifruit slices on top and sprinkle with some of honey mixture. Top with a second crepe. Repeat until all the crepes are used, finishing with a crepe on top. Whip cream until soft peaks form; fold in remaining liqueur. Spoon into a piping bag fitted with an open-star tip. Cut gâteau in wedges and pipe rosettes of cream on each wedge. Arrange any remaining mandarin oranges and kiwifruit slices on top. Serve immediately. Serves 4.

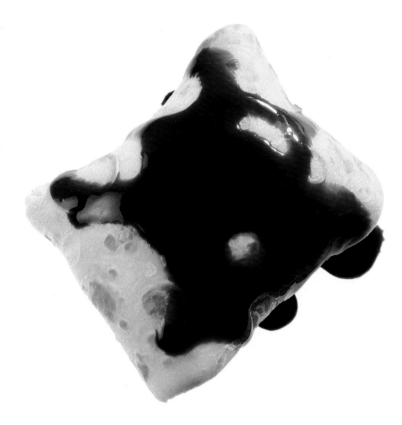

— Ice Cream Crepes & Chocolate Sauce —

Chocolate Sauce:
2/3 cup water
1/2 cup sugar
1/2 cup unsweetened cocoa powder

7-inch crepes (page 12, 13, 14 or 15)

1 pint vanilla ice cream
2 tablespoons cherry brandy

For sauce: Combine water and sugar in a small saucepan. Place over low heat and stir until sugar is dissolved. Bring to a boil, then simmer 1 minute. Add cocoa and return to boil, whisking constantly until sauce is smooth. Keep warm.

Cut ice cream into 8 cubes; wrap each one in a crepe. Arrange two crepes on each plate. Sprinkle with cherry brandy. Top with Chocolate Sauce and serve immediately. Serves 4.

— Apple-Raisin Crepes with Rum Sauce —

Rum Sauce:
1/4 cup unsalted butter
2/3 cup brown sugar
3 tablespoons whipping cream
1/4 cup dark rum

7-inch crepes (page 12, 13, 14 or 15)

1 (8-oz.) pkg. cream cheese, room
  temperature
3/4 cup raisins
1 eating apple, peeled and sliced
Cinnamon

For Sauce: In a small bowl, cream butter and sugar until light and fluffy. Beat in cream and rum. Transfer to a serving bowl.

Keep crepes warm while preparing filling. In a small bowl, beat cream cheese until light and fluffy. Stir in raisins and apple (reserve some of apple for garnish, if desired). Divide mixture between crepes. Roll up lightly and arrange in single layer in serving dish. Decorate with apple and sprinkle with cinnamon. Serve with Rum Sauce. Serves 4.

Viennese Crepes

Chocolate Sauce (page 65)

7-inch crepes (page 12, 13, 14 or 15)

1/3 cup unsalted butter
1/2 cup powdered sugar
2 tablespoons ground almonds
1 tablespoon strong coffee, cooled

Make Chocolate Sauce and keep warm. In a small bowl, cream butter until light and fluffy. Add sugar, almonds and coffee and beat until light and creamy.

Divide mixture between crepes. Fold into quarters and arrange two crepes on each plate. Pour Chocolate Sauce into a serving bowl or pitcher and pass separately. Serves 4.

Basic Waffles

1-1/2 cups all-purpose flour
2 teaspoons baking powder
1/2 teaspoon salt
2 teaspoons sugar
2 eggs, separated
1 cup milk
1/3 cup butter, melted
Butter and maple syrup *or* bacon

Sift flour, baking powder and salt into a medium-size bowl. Stir in sugar. In another bowl, combine egg yolks, milk and butter and beat well. Add to dry ingredients and beat thoroughly. In another bowl, beat egg whites until stiff. Fold into batter.

Heat waffle iron, but do not grease. To test for correct heat, put 1 teaspoon water inside waffle iron, close and heat. When steaming stops, heat is correct for cooking waffles. Spoon 1 tablespoon batter into center of each compartment. Close and cook until puffed and golden brown. Lift out waffles with a fork. Serve hot with butter and maple syrup, or with bacon. Alternatively, serve waffles sandwiched together with whipped cream and decorated with fruit and powdered sugar. Makes 6 waffles.

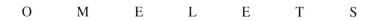

Crispy Cheese Waffles

1-1/2 cups all-purpose flour
2 teaspoons baking powder
1/2 teaspoon salt
2 eggs, separated
1 cup milk
1/3 cup butter, melted
1/2 cup (2 oz.) shredded Cheddar cheese
Cream cheese, sliced apples and bacon

Sift flour, baking powder and salt into a medium-size bowl. In another bowl, combine egg yolks, milk and butter and beat well. Add to dry ingredients along with cheese and beat thoroughly. In another bowl, beat egg whites until stiff. Fold into batter.

Heat waffle iron, but do not grease. To test for correct heat, put 1 teaspoon water inside waffle iron, close and heat. When steaming stops, heat is correct for cooking waffles. Spoon 1 tablespoon batter into center of each compartment. Close and cook until puffed and golden brown. Lift out waffles with a fork. Serve hot with cream cheese, sliced apples and bacon. Makes 6 waffles.

Chocolate Cream Waffles

2/3 cup whipping cream
1-1/2 cups all-purpose flour
2 teaspoons baking powder
1/2 teaspoon salt
2 tablespoons sugar
2 eggs, separated
1 cup milk
1/3 cup butter, melted
2 oz. (2 squares) sweet dark chocolate,
   melted and cooled
1/2 teaspoon vanilla
Whipped cream and grated chocolate to
   decorate

In a small bowl, beat cream until soft peaks form. Spoon into serving bowl and refrigerate. Sift flour, baking powder and salt into a medium-size bowl. Stir in sugar. In another bowl, combine egg yolks, milk, butter, chocolate and vanilla and beat well. Add to dry ingredients and beat thoroughly. In another bowl, beat egg whites until stiff. Fold into batter.

Heat waffle iron, but do not grease. To test for correct heat, put 1 teaspoon water inside waffle iron, close and heat. When steaming stops, heat is correct for cooking waffles. Spoon 1 tablespoon batter into center of each compartment. Close and cook until puffed and crisp. Lift out waffles with a fork. Decorate with whipped cream and grated chocolate. Makes 6 waffles.

—————— Banana Nut Waffles ——————

1-1/2 cups all-purpose flour
2 teaspoons baking powder
1/2 teaspoon salt
2 teaspoons sugar
2 eggs, separated
1 cup milk
1/3 cup butter, melted
3/4 cup finely chopped walnuts
2 medium-size bananas
2 tablespoons powdered sugar
1 tablespoon lemon juice

Sift flour, baking powder and salt into a medium-size bowl. Stir in sugar. In another bowl, combine egg yolks, milk and butter and beat well. Add to dry ingredients and beat thoroughly. Stir in 1 tablespoon of the walnuts. In another bowl, beat egg whites until stiff. Fold into batter.

Heat waffle iron, but do not grease. To test for correct heat, put 1 teaspoon water inside waffle iron, close and heat. When steaming stops, heat is correct for cooking waffles. Spoon 1 tablespoon batter into center of each compartment. Close and cook until puffed and golden brown. While waffles are cooking, peel bananas; slice into a bowl and sprinkle with sugar and lemon juice. Lift out waffles with a fork. Serve hot, topped with banana slices and sprinkled with remaining nuts. Makes 6 waffles.

Apricot-Cream Waffles

6 Basic Waffles (page 68)

1 (8-oz.) can apricots in syrup
3 tablespoons orange marmalade
1 tablespoon brandy
2/3 cup whipping cream
2 oz. (1/2 cup) slivered almonds, toasted

While waffles are cooking, prepare topping. Combine undrained apricots, marmalade and brandy in blender or food processor. Blend to a smooth puree. Pour into serving bowl.

In a small bowl, beat cream until soft peaks form. Serve waffles hot topped with apricot puree and sprinkled with almonds. Pass whipped cream separately. Serves 6.

Strawberry-Rum Waffles

6 Basic Waffles (page 68)

8 oz. fresh strawberries, thickly sliced
1/4 cup sugar
2 tablespoons light rum
6 scoops strawberry ice cream

While waffles are cooking, prepare topping. In a small bowl, combine strawberries, sugar and rum. Stir well and set aside until waffles are ready.

Spoon strawberries and liquid over hot waffles. Top each one with a scoop of ice cream. Serves 6.

OMELET TECHNIQUES

There are three basic types of omelets. They may be cooked over direct heat, or adapted to baking in the oven or the microwave.

The French Omelet, which is also called a plain omelet, is like a thick, soft, golden pillow, which may be flavored or filled.

The Soufflé Omelet is also known as a fluffy or puffy omelet. It is made by beating egg yolks separately and then folding in stiffly beaten egg whites. This results in a light, soufflé-like mixture, which collapses quickly, and is most often used for sweet omelets.

The Spanish Omelet (Tortilla) is a thick omelet with vegetables and/or meat, poultry or fish cooked in the beaten eggs. This omelet is not folded, but cut into wedges.

Ingredients

An omelet simply consists of beaten eggs cooked in butter. Eggs weighing 2 ounces (labeled "large") are the best size to use. A 3-egg omelet is enough for 1 person, but with a substantial filling, it can serve two. A 5- or 6-egg omelet will also serve two, but a filling will extend the mixture to serve three.

If 1 teaspoon water is added to each egg the omelet will be light, but this is not necessary; milk should *not* be added as this makes the egg mixture heavier. For cooking, use 1 tablespoon butter (or slightly less) for 3 eggs.

Flavorings and Fillings

The rich mixture of eggs and butter needs no additional enhancement other than salt and pepper, but omelets are a natural for numerous other flavorings. For example, chopped fresh herbs may be added, allowing 1 tablespoon herbs to 3 eggs. Cheese may also be used, allowing 1/2 cup (2 ounces) diced or shredded cheese to 3 eggs.

Chopped ham or cream cheese may be folded into the basic uncooked omelet, or fillings such as cooked mushrooms or bacon may be added to the cooked omelet. Fish, shellfish, poultry, game or ham may also be added to a white sauce or cheese sauce and used as a filling.

Basic Preparation and Serving

Always use fresh ingredients, and only prepare an omelet just before serving. Break eggs into a bowl and beat lightly with a fork—*not* a whisk; the eggs should only be very lightly mixed together. If eggs are overbeaten, a thin watery omelet will result.

Before cooking, warm serving plates, and preheat the oven if necessary; if the broiler will be needed, preheat shortly before using. Place the omelet pan—typically a 7- to 8-inch pan with sloping sides—over low heat to become thoroughly hot. Add the butter and, when it sizzles but is not browned, add the eggs.

Using a fork or spatula, draw the mixture from the sides to the middle of the pan, allowing the uncooked egg to run underneath and cook quickly. Repeat this process two or three times so all the egg sets, rises slightly and becomes fluffy, not flat. Cook only about 2 minutes, until the base is lightly golden and the top still slightly runny (the eggs continue cooking when removed from heat). Remove from heat.

If filling an omelet, make a little cut on opposite sides of the cooked mixture. Add filling to one half, fold the other half over, and lift or flip onto a warm plate. The filling should be precooked and warm.

Baked and Microwaved Omelets

Omelets may be baked about 10 minutes in a slow—325F (165C)— oven. This is a good method for a filled omelet that will be served flat. An omelet pan with an ovenproof handle is best to use, as the base of the omelet should be lightly cooked over direct heat before finishing in the oven.

Omelets may be successfully cooked in a microwave oven on full power—about 2 minutes for the 3-egg size. The butter should be melted 30 seconds in a shallow 7-inch, microwave-safe dish before the eggs are added. After 1 minute of microwaving, lift eggs from the sides with a fork, then continue microwaving 1 minute.

Omelet Fondante

A very rich plain omelet may be made by adding 1 tablespoon half and half and 1 tablespoon diced butter to the beaten eggs. As the omelet cooks, the butter melts into little pockets to give extra flavor and richness.

Folding and Serving Omelets

To fold a plain omelet use a metal spatula and fold over 1/3 of cooked mixture *away* from handle. Hold the handle with the palm of the hand on top and place the pan over a warm plate. Shake omelet to edge of pan and tip completely over to make another fold. If desired, quickly drop a piece of butter on top of the hot omelet and spread over the surface to give a beautiful glaze.

Spanish omelets, or those with a lot of filling in the sauce, may be served flat, without folding, and cut into wedges. They may be placed under a broiler just long enough to lightly brown the filling or set the top.

Basic Omelet

3 eggs
Salt and pepper
1 tablespoon butter

In a small bowl, beat eggs with salt and pepper until just mixed. Set 7-inch omelet pan over low heat to become thoroughly hot.

Add butter to pan. When butter is sizzling but not brown, pour in eggs. Using a fork or spatula, draw mixture from sides to middle of pan, allowing uncooked egg to run underneath. Repeat two or three times so egg rises slightly and becomes fluffy. Cook until golden-brown underneath and top is still slightly runny, about 2 minutes.

Using a metal spatula, fold over 1/3 of mixture away from handle. Holding the handle with the palm of the hand on top, place the pan over a warm serving plate. Shake omelet to edge of pan and tip completely over to make another fold. Garnish with a sprig of watercress and a tomato wedge, if desired. Serve immediately. Serves 1.

Smoked Salmon Omelets

6 eggs
Salt and pepper
2 tablespoons butter
4 oz. smoked salmon, finely chopped
1 teaspoon chopped fresh parsley
1 teaspoon chopped fresh chives
Additional smoked salmon and chives

In a medium-size bowl, beat eggs with salt and pepper until just mixed. Set 7-inch omelet pan or small skillet over low heat to become thoroughly hot. Add a little butter to pan. When butter is sizzling but not brown, add 2 tablespoons of the egg and cook until just set. Lift onto a baking sheet and keep warm. Repeat until all eggs are cooked.

Mix salmon with parsley and chives. Spoon onto one half of each small omelet. Fold over and garnish with additional salmon and chives. Serve immediately. Serves 4.

Seafood Soufflé Omelet

3 eggs, separated
Salt and pepper
2 tablespoons butter
4 oz. peeled and deveined cooked shrimp
1 tablespoon lemon juice
1 teaspoon chili sauce
Lemon slices and fennel or dill sprigs

In a medium-size bowl, beat egg yolks, salt and pepper. In another bowl, beat egg whites until stiff. Fold into yolks. Set 7-inch omelet pan or small skillet over low heat to become thoroughly hot. Add half the butter. When butter is sizzling but not brown, pour in eggs and cook until base is golden-brown, 2 to 3 minutes.

While omelet is cooking, preheat broiler and prepare filling. Heat remaining butter in a small skillet. Add shrimp, lemon juice and chili sauce and heat through. Transfer omelet to broiler until lightly browned, about 30 seconds. Spoon filling over half the omelet. Fold over, cut in half and garnish with lemon and herb sprig. Serve immediately. Serves 2.

Curried Omelet

2 tablespoons butter
1 medium-size onion, finely chopped
2 teaspoons curry powder
1 eating apple, peeled, cored and diced
1 tablespoon mango chutney, finely
  chopped
Salt and pepper
Squeeze of lemon juice

Basic Omelet (page 76)

Prepare filling before making omelet.
Melt butter in a medium-size skillet over
low heat. Add onion and cook 3 minutes.
Stir in curry powder and apple and continue cooking, stirring occasionally, 5 minutes. Stir in chutney. Season with salt,
pepper and lemon juice. Keep warm.

Make omelet. Spoon filling over half the
omelet. Fold over, cut in half and serve
immediately. Garnish with apple slices
and coriander sprigs, if desired. Serves 2.

Arnold Bennett Omelet

3 eggs
6 oz. smoked cod or haddock fillets,
  cooked and flaked
Salt and pepper
2 tablespoons butter
5 tablespoons half and half
1/2 cup (2 oz.) shredded Cheddar cheese
Lemon twists and chopped parsley

In a small bowl, beat eggs until just mixed. Stir in fish. Season with salt and pepper. Set 7-inch omelet pan over low heat to become thoroughly hot. Add butter to pan. When butter is sizzling but not brown, pour in eggs. Using a fork or spatula, draw mixture from sides to middle of pan, allowing uncooked egg to run underneath. Repeat two or three times until egg rises slightly and becomes fluffy. Cook until golden-brown underneath and top is still slightly runny, about 2 minutes. Lift onto warm heatproof plate.

Preheat broiler. Cover omelet with half and half and sprinkle with cheese. Broil several inches from heat source until top is golden and bubbling. Garnish with lemon twists and parsley. Do not fold; serve immediately. Serves 2.

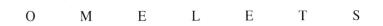

Italian Omelet

Filling:
4 tablespoons butter
1 small onion, finely chopped
1 medium-size tomato, peeled and
chopped
1 tablespoon chopped green pepper

Omelet:
3 eggs
2 oz. (1/3 cup) cooked pasta
Salt and pepper
2 tablespoons grated Parmesan cheese
Basil leaves

Prepare filling before making omelet. Melt 2 tablespoons butter in a small saucepan over low heat. Add onion and cook, stirring occasionally, 2 minutes. Stir in tomato and green pepper. Cover and cook 10 minutes.

Preheat broiler. In a small bowl, beat eggs until just mixed. Stir in pasta. Season with salt and pepper. Set 7-inch omelet pan over low heat to become thoroughly hot. Add remaining butter to pan. When butter is sizzling but not brown, pour in egg mixture. Using a fork or spatula, draw mixture from sides to middle of pan, allowing uncooked egg to run underneath. Repeat two or three times until egg rises slightly and becomes fluffy. Cook until golden-brown underneath and top is slightly runny, about 2 minutes.

Spread filling over half the omelet. Fold over and sprinkle with Parmesan. Broil just long enough to melt cheese, about 30 seconds. To serve, cut in half and garnish with basil. Serves 2.

Chicken Liver Omelet

1 tablespoon butter
4 oz. chicken livers, coarsely chopped
1 small onion, finely chopped
1 teaspoon all-purpose flour
2 tablespoons chicken broth
2 teaspoons fresh chopped thyme
Salt and pepper

Basic Omelet (page 76)

Prepare filling before making omelet. Melt butter in a small skillet over low heat. Add chicken livers and onion and stir until onion is soft and golden, about 3 minutes. Stir in flour, broth and thyme. Bring to boil, then simmer 10 minutes. Season with salt and pepper.

Make omelet. Spoon filling over half the omelet. Fold over and serve immediately. Garnish with sprigs of thyme and grapes, if desired. Serves 1.

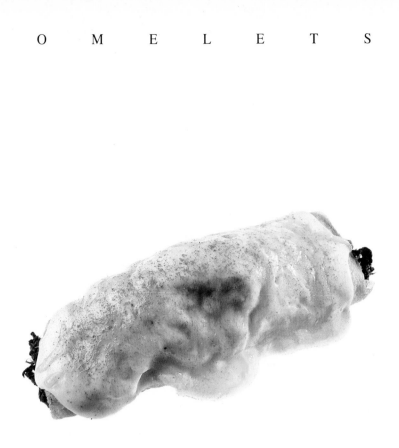

Florentine Omelet

4 oz. fresh spinach, well-washed

1/2 recipe Cheese Sauce (page 23)

Basic Omelet (page 76)

1/2 cup (2 oz.) shredded Cheddar cheese
Cayenne pepper

Prepare filling before making omelet. Cook spinach in a small saucepan over low heat until very tender. Drain well; press out excess moisture. Warm Cheese Sauce.

Preheat broiler. Make omelet. Spoon spinach over half the omelet. Fold over and lift onto a warm heatproof plate. Spoon Cheese Sauce over top; sprinkle with cheese and cayenne. Broil until sauce is bubbling and lightly browned. Serves 1.

Tortilla Loaf

4 lean slices bacon, chopped
1 tablespoon butter
1/2 lb. potatoes, cooked and diced
6 eggs
Salt and pepper
4 long bread rolls
Butter
Lettuce leaves

In a medium-size skillet over medium-high heat, combine bacon and butter. Cook until bacon is soft. Reduce heat to medium, stir in potatoes and cook until golden. In a medium-size bowl, beat eggs with salt and pepper until just mixed. Pour over potatoes and cook, lifting with a fork, until eggs are just set.

Split rolls lengthwise; spread cut sides lightly with butter. Place a lettuce leaf on bottom half of each roll. Cut egg mixture into slices and place on lettuce. Cover with top half of roll. Serve hot or cold. Serves 4.

———— Garlic Crouton Omelet ————

1 slice white bread, crusts trimmed
2 tablespoons butter
1 tablespoon vegetable oil
1 garlic clove, crushed
Salt and pepper

Basic Omelet (page 76)

Prepare filling before making omelet. Cut
bread into 1/2-inch cubes. Heat butter and
oil in a small skillet over medium heat.
Stir in garlic. Add bread cubes and fry
until crisp and golden. Drain well. Season
with salt and pepper.

Make omelet. Sprinkle croutons over half
the omelet. Fold over and serve immediately. Garnish with celery leaves
and extra croutons, if desired. Serves 1.

Potato & Herb Omelet

1 tablespoon vegetable oil
1 large potato, cooked and thinly sliced
1 teaspoon chopped fresh rosemary
1 teaspoon chopped fresh chervil
Salt and pepper

Basic Omelet (page 76)

Prepare filling before making omelet. Heat oil in a large skillet over medium-high heat. Add potato slices in a single layer. Fry until crisp and golden. Drain very well. Add rosemary and chervil and season generously with salt and pepper. Toss well.

Make omelet. Spoon potato mixture over half the omelet. Fold over and serve immediately. Garnish with sprigs of rosemary and chervil, if desired. Serves 1.

Ham & Watercress Omelet

1 tablespoon butter
2 oz. (1/4 cup) cooked ham, finely
   chopped
1/4 cup finely chopped watercress leaves
Salt and pepper

Basic Omelet (page 76)

Prepare filling before making omelet.
Melt butter in a small skillet over low
heat. Add ham and watercress and shake
until warmed through, about 1 minute.
Remove from heat and season well with
salt and pepper.

Make omelet. Spoon ham mixture over
half the omelet. Fold over and serve immediately. Garnish with a sprig of watercress and rolls of thickly-sliced ham, if
desired. Serves 1.

Bacon & Mushroom Omelet

1 tablespoon butter
2 lean slices bacon, diced
3/4 cup thinly sliced mushrooms
3 eggs
Salt and pepper
1 medium-size tomato, peeled and sliced

Melt butter in a 7-inch omelet pan over low heat. Add bacon and cook 2 minutes. Stir in mushrooms and cook 2 minutes.

In a small bowl, beat eggs with salt and pepper until just mixed. Pour into pan with bacon and mushrooms and top with tomato slices. As eggs cook, draw the mixture from edge of pan to center so uncooked egg runs underneath. When top is just set, slide omelet flat onto serving plate. Garnish with a sprig of mint and mushroom slices, if desired. Serves 1.

Fluffy Cheese Omelet

3 eggs, separated
Salt and pepper
1 tablespoon butter
1/2 cup (2 oz.) Red Leicester cheese,
  shredded

In a medium-size bowl, beat egg yolks
with salt and pepper until creamy. In another bowl, beat egg whites until stiff.
Fold into yolks. Set 7-inch omelet pan
over low heat to become thoroughly hot.
Add butter. When butter is sizzling but
not brown, add eggs. Cook until golden-
brown underneath, 2 to 3 minutes.

Preheat broiler. Lift omelet onto a warm
heatproof plate. Sprinkle about 3/4 of the
cheese over surface. Fold omelet in half;
sprinkle remaining cheese on top. Broil
until cheese is melted, about 30 seconds.
Garnish with a sprig of chervil, if desired.
Serve immediately. Serves 1.

Basic Soufflé Omelet

3 eggs, separated
1 tablespoon sugar
1 tablespoon butter

Filling (see below)

Preheat broiler. In a medium-size bowl, beat egg yolks and sugar until thick, pale and creamy. In another bowl, beat egg whites until stiff. Fold into yolks. Set 7-inch omelet pan over medium heat. Add butter and heat briefly. Reduce heat to low. Pour in egg mixture and level off lightly. Cook until bottom is set and pale golden-brown. Broil omelet several inches from heat source until top is lightly browned.

Spread filling on half of omelet. Fold over and serve immediately.

For filling: Use sliced fresh fruit, lightly sweetened and flavored with liqueur, or, as an alternative, fill omelet with a little hot jam, marmalade or honey, which may be mixed with finely chopped nuts. Serves 2.

Omelet-Meringue Surprise

6 eggs
2 tablespoons sugar
2 almond macaroons, crushed
2 tablespoons half and half
1 tablespoon butter
5 tablespoons blackberry or black
    currant jam
1/4 cup finely chopped walnuts

Topping:
2 egg whites
1/2 cup sugar
2 tablespoons powdered sugar, sifted

Preheat oven to 425F (220C). In a medium-size bowl, beat eggs, sugar, macaroons and half and half until thick and creamy. Set 7-inch omelet pan over low heat to become thoroughly hot. Add half the butter and heat until sizzling but not brown. Pour in half the egg mixture. Cook until just set. Lift onto a warm heat-proof plate. Repeat with remaining butter and egg mixture. Warm jam in a small saucepan over low heat. Stir in walnuts. Spread over first omelet; top with second omelet.

For topping: In a bowl, beat egg whites until stiff; gradually beat in sugar. Pipe meringue over omelets, *sealing completely* (do not leave even a pin-sized area unsealed or meringue will begin to shrink). Sprinkle with powdered sugar. Bake 3 minutes. Serve immediately. Serves 4.

Christmas Omelet

6 eggs, separated
2 tablespoons sugar
Grated zest (colored part only) of 1
   orange
4 tablespoons rum
2 tablespoons butter
6 tablespoons fruit mincemeat
2 teaspoons powdered sugar, sifted

In a medium-size bowl, beat egg yolks with sugar, zest and 1 tablespoon of the rum. In a large bowl, beat egg whites until stiff. Fold into yolks. Set an 8-inch omelet pan over low heat to become thoroughly hot. Add butter and heat until sizzling but not brown. Add egg mixture; cook until golden-brown underneath, 4 to 5 minutes.

Preheat broiler. Heat mincemeat in a small saucepan until lukewarm. Spread on half the omelet. Fold over and lift onto a warm heatproof plate. Sprinkle with powdered sugar. Broil until sugar is melted and top is glazed, about 30 seconds. In a small pan, gently warm remaining rum. Pour over omelet and ignite quickly with a match. Serves 3 to 4.

Summer Soufflé Omelet

6 oz. mixed fruits such as black currants,
  red currants, raspberries and
  strawberries
3 tablespoons crème de cassis or water
1 tablespoon sugar
1 tablespoon arrowroot

Basic Soufflé Omelet (page 90)

1 tablespoon powdered sugar, sifted

Prepare filling before making omelet. Put fruit in a medium-size saucepan with crème de cassis and sugar. Cook over medium heat until juices run. Remove from heat. Mix arrowroot with a little water then stir into fruit. Return to heat and cook, stirring, until thickened. Let cool.

Prepare omelet and place on a warm heat-proof plate. Spoon cooled filling over half the omelet and fold over. Sprinkle with powdered sugar. Decorate with fruit and leaves, if desired. Serves 2.

Sweet Pineapple Omelet

1 (8-oz.) can pineapple tidbits in juice
1 teaspoon arrowroot or cornstarch
2 teaspoons water
**2 teaspoons grated lemon zest (colored
    part only)**
2 teaspoons fresh chopped mint

Basic Soufflé Omelet (page 90)

Prepare filling before making omelet.
Drain pineapple, reserving 3 tablespoons
juice; finely chop pineapple. In a small
saucepan, bring reserved juice to a boil.
Mix arrowroot with water and stir into
juice. Reduce heat and cook gently, stirring often, until mixture is clear. Stir in
pineapple, zest and mint. Remove from
heat.

Make omelet. Lift onto warm serving
plate. Spoon pineapple over half the omelet. Fold over and serve immediately.
Garnish with lemon twists and mint
sprigs, if desired. Serves 2.

Soufflé Omelet Surprise

2-1/2 cups vanilla ice cream
8 oz. raspberries or strawberries
2 tablespoons kirsch
2 tablespoons sugar
1 thin, 8- or 9-inch sponge cake
3 eggs, separated
Sugar

Before proceeding with recipe, line 8- or 9-inch cake pan (use same size as sponge cake) with plastic wrap; spoon in ice cream, spreading evenly. Freeze until very hard. Preheat oven to 425F (220C). Reserve a few raspberries or strawberries for decoration. Leave remaining raspberries whole or slice remaining strawberries if using instead. Combine berries with kirsch and 1 tablespoon sugar in a small bowl. Place sponge cake on flat heatproof plate. Spoon fruit and juice over cake.

In a medium-size bowl, beat egg yolks with remaining 1 tablespoon sugar until thick and creamy. In another bowl, beat egg whites until stiff. Fold into yolks. Remove ice cream by lifting edges of plastic wrap; peel off plastic. Set ice cream over berries. Quickly spread egg mixture over ice cream and cake, covering completely. Sprinkle with sugar. Bake 3 minutes. Decorate with reserved raspberries or strawberries and serve immediately. Serves 6.

Blackberry Soufflé Omelet

3 eggs, separated
2 tablespoons sugar
3 tablespoons butter
1/2 cup blackberries
2/3 cup whipping cream

In a medium-size bowl, beat egg yolks and 1 tablespoon sugar until thick and creamy. In another bowl, beat egg whites until stiff. Fold into yolks. Set 7-inch omelet pan over low heat to become thoroughly hot. Add 2 tablespoons butter and heat until sizzling but not brown. Pour in egg mixture and cook until golden-brown underneath, 2 to 3 minutes. Preheat broiler.

While omelet is cooking, combine blackberries with remaining sugar and butter in a small saucepan. Place over low heat and bring to a simmer for 2 minutes. Transfer omelet to broiler and arrange several inches from heat source. Broil until top is lightly browned. Lift onto a warm serving dish and top with berries. In a small bowl, beat cream until soft peaks form. Pipe over each serving. Use blackberry leaves to garnish, if desired. Serves 2.

Fruit Salad Fluffy Omelet

2 medium-size eating apples, peeled and
    diced
1 medium-size banana, thinly sliced
1 medium-size orange
3 eggs, separated
2 tablespoons sugar
1 tablespoon butter
2 teaspoons powdered sugar, sifted
Orange wedges and mint leaves

Combine apples and banana in a bowl.
Peel orange and remove all white pith.
Cut crosswise into thin slices; cut each
slice into quarters and add to bowl. In a
medium-size bowl, beat egg yolks until
pale and creamy. Stir in fruit. In another
bowl, beat egg whites until stiff; gradually beat in sugar. Fold into fruit mixture.

Preheat broiler. Melt butter in an 8-inch
omelet pan over low heat. Add egg mixture and cook until base is golden-brown,
2 to 3 minutes. Broil briefly just until top
is lightly browned. Sprinkle with powdered sugar. Gently cut omelet into quarters. Serve from pan as omelet is very
tender and breaks easily. Garnish with
oranges and mint. Serves 4.

Cherry Soufflé Omelet

Filling:
1/4 cup sugar
2/3 cup water
4 oz. (about 2/3 cup) black cherries,
pitted, halved

Omelet:
3 eggs, separated
2 tablespoons sugar
1 tablespoon butter

For filling: Combine sugar and water in small pan and heat gently until sugar is dissolved. Bring to a boil. Add cherries and cook until just soft, about 3 minutes. Remove from heat.

For omelet: Preheat broiler. In a medium-size bowl, beat egg yolks with 1 tablespoon sugar. In another bowl, beat egg whites until stiff. Fold into yolks. Melt butter in a 7-inch omelet pan over low heat. Pour in egg mixture and cook, loosening edges, until fluffy and lightly browned underneath. Broil until top is lightly browned. Spoon cherries and half the syrup over omelet. Fold in half. Sprinkle with remaining sugar. Serves 2.

Sweet & Sharp Omelet

6 eggs, separated
2/3 cup sour cream
2 teaspoons lemon juice
1/2 teaspoon grated lemon zest
1/2 teaspoon salt
2 tablespoons butter
2 teaspoons sugar
4 tablespoons cherry or strawberry jam
2/3 cup sour cream

In a medium-size bowl, beat egg yolks, 2/3 cup sour cream, lemon juice, lemon zest and salt until well mixed. In a large bowl, beat egg whites until stiff. Fold into yolks. Preheat broiler. Melt butter in an 8-inch omelet pan over low heat. Pour in egg mixture and cook, loosening edges, until lightly browned underneath.

Broil briefly until top is lightly browned. Sprinkle with sugar. Cut omelet into quarters. Top each with a tablespoon of jam and a dollop of sour cream. Serves 4.

Friar's Omelet

2 slices white bread
1/4 cup butter
2 medium-size tomatoes, peeled and
   chopped
6 eggs
1/2 teaspoon chopped mixed fresh herbs
Salt and pepper

Preheat oven to 325F (165C). Trim crusts from bread; cut bread into 1/2-inch cubes. Melt butter in an 8-inch omelet pan over medium heat. Add bread and fry, stirring frequently, until lightly browned. Add tomatoes and cook 1 minute.

In a medium-size bowl, beat eggs with herbs, salt and pepper until just mixed. Add eggs to pan and cook 1 minute, using a fork or spatula to draw mixture from sides to middle of pan so uncooked egg runs underneath. Transfer to oven and bake 10 minutes. Garnish with whole chives, if desired. This omelet is good served hot or cold. Serves 2 to 3.

Puffy Cottage Cheese Omelet

4 eggs, separated
1 cup (8 oz.) cottage cheese
Salt and pepper
2 tablespoons butter
2 medium-size tomatoes, peeled and
    sliced
Sprigs of parsley

Preheat oven to 325F (165C). In a medium-size bowl, beat egg yolks lightly. Add cottage cheese, salt and pepper and beat well. In another bowl, beat egg whites until stiff. Fold into egg mixture. Melt butter in an 8-inch omelet pan over low heat. Pour in egg mixture, spreading lightly. Cook 1 minute.

Arrange tomato slices in a single layer on top of omelet. Transfer to oven and bake 10 minutes. Do not fold this omelet. Garnish with parsley sprigs. Serves 2.

Deviled Ham Omelet

5 eggs
1/2 teaspoon dry mustard
1/4 teaspoon curry powder
Salt and pepper
2/3 cup sour cream
3 tablespoons water
1 cup finely chopped cooked ham
2 tablespoons butter
Parsley sprigs

Preheat oven to 325F (165C). In a medium-size bowl, beat eggs with mustard, curry, salt and pepper. Add half the sour cream and all the water and beat until well mixed. Stir in 1/2 cup ham.

Melt butter in an 8-inch omelet pan over low heat. Pour in egg mixture and cook 1 minute, using a fork or spatula to draw mixture from sides to middle of pan so uncooked egg runs underneath. Transfer to oven and bake 10 minutes. Mix remaining sour cream and ham and spoon over omelet. Garnish with parsley sprigs and serve immediately. Serves 2.

Sunday Omelet

1 chicken liver, coarsely chopped
2 lean slices bacon, diced
1 small onion, finely chopped
2 tablespoons butter
1 large potato, cooked and diced
2 tablespoons cooked peas
4 eggs
Salt and pepper
2 tablespoons butter
Parsley sprig and tomato slices

Preheat oven to 325F (165C). Combine liver and bacon in an 8-inch omelet pan. Cook over low heat until liver is just colored and bacon is softened. Add onion and cook until lightly colored, 2 to 3 minutes. Add 2 tablespoons butter and potato and cook until potatoes are golden. Stir in peas.

In a bowl, beat eggs with salt and pepper. Add remaining butter to pan. When melted, pour in eggs and cook 1 minute. Transfer to oven and bake 10 minutes. Do not fold this omelet. Garnish with parsley sprig and tomato slices. Serves 2 to 3.

Savory Soufflé Omelet

5 eggs, separated
Salt and pepper
2 tablespoons butter
6 green onions, finely chopped

1/2 recipe Cheese Sauce (page 23)

1/4 cup (1 oz.) shredded Cheddar cheese

Preheat oven to 325F (165C). In a medium-size bowl, beat egg yolks with salt and pepper until creamy. In a large bowl, beat egg whites until stiff. Fold into yolks. Melt butter in an 8-inch omelet pan over low heat. Pour in egg mixture, spreading lightly. Cook 1 minute.

Sprinkle omelet with onions. Transfer to oven and bake 5 minutes. Quickly spoon on Cheese Sauce and sprinkle with cheese. Continue baking 5 minutes. Do not fold this omelet. Garnish with a green onion, if desired. Serves 2.

Fluffy Chicken Omelet

5 eggs, separated
Salt and pepper
2 teaspoons chopped fresh parsley
2 tablespoons butter
4 oz. (1 cup) cooked chicken, diced
1 medium-size tomato, peeled and sliced

Preheat oven to 325 (165C). In a medium-size bowl, beat egg yolks with salt and pepper until creamy. Stir in parsley. In another bowl, beat egg whites until stiff. Fold into egg mixture. Melt butter in an 8-inch omelet pan over low heat. Pour in egg mixture and cook 1 minute.

Top with chicken. Transfer to oven and bake 5 minutes. Arrange tomato slices over half the omelet. Fold over and continue baking 5 minutes. Garnish with small sprigs of parsley, if desired. To serve, cut in half. Serves 2.

—— Shrimp & Mushroom Omelet ——

4 tablespoons butter
2 oz. mushrooms, thinly sliced
1 tablespoon all-purpose flour
2/3 cup milk
1 cup (4 oz.) cooked, peeled shrimp
2 oz. cooked mussels (optional)
Salt and pepper
5 eggs
Whole chives

Preheat oven to 325F (165C). Melt 2 tablespoons butter in small skillet over medium heat. Add mushrooms and cook 1 minute. Stir in flour and cook 30 seconds. Gradually stir in milk and bring to a boil. Stir in shrimp, mussels, salt and pepper. Remove from heat.

In a medium-size bowl, beat eggs with salt and pepper until just mixed. Melt remaining 2 tablespoons butter in an 8-inch omelet pan over low heat. Pour in egg mixture and cook 1 minute. Transfer to oven and bake 5 minutes. Top with shrimp mixture and bake 5 minutes. Do not fold this omelet. Garnish with chives. Serves 2.

Omelet Lorraine

2 tablespoons butter
4 oz. (1 cup) uncooked ham, diced
6 eggs
Salt and pepper
1/2 cup (2 oz.) shredded Gruyère, Samsø
  or Tybo cheese
1 teaspoon chopped fresh chives

Preheat oven to 325F (165C). Melt 1 tablespoon butter in an 8-inch omelet pan over low heat. Add ham and cook until completely done.

In a medium-size bowl, beat eggs with salt and pepper until just mixed. Stir in cheese and chives. Add remaining butter to pan. When melted, pour egg mixture over ham and cook 1 minute. Transfer to oven and bake 10 minutes. Do not fold this omelet. Garnish with chives, if desired. Serves 2.

Russian Batter Omelet

1 cup half and half
3/4 cup (3 oz.) all-purpose flour
6 eggs
Salt and pepper
1/2 cup butter
2 oz. smoked salmon, cut in strips

Preheat oven to 400F (205C). In a medium-size bowl, beat half and half and flour together until smooth. Add eggs one at a time, beating well after each addition. Season well with salt and pepper. Beat vigorously until creamy.

Melt butter in an 8-inch omelet pan over low heat. Pour in batter and cook 2 minutes. Transfer to oven and bake 8 minutes. Top with smoked salmon and serve immediately. Do not fold this omelet. If desired, garnish with a slice of lemon, a sprig of dill and a salmon cone filled with caviar. Serves 3.

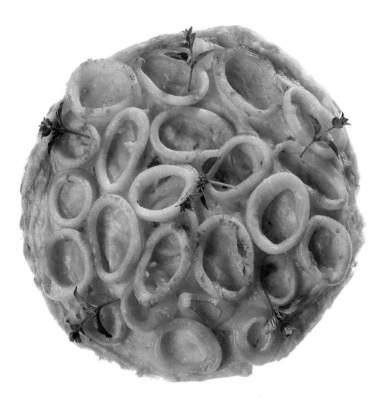

Italian Squid Omelet

1/2 lb. squid

3 tablespoons vegetable oil
1 garlic clove, crushed
2 tablespoons butter
6 eggs
Salt and pepper

Preheat oven to 325F (165C). Pull tentacles from squid, removing stomach and ink bag with them; set aside. Wash body of squid; peel off skin. Cut beak and ink bag from tentacles and discard; wash tentacles well. Partially fill medium-size saucepan with water and bring to a boil. Add body and tentacles and return water to boil. Drain and rinse squid in cold water. Slice into rings. Pat dry.

Heat oil with garlic in an 8-inch omelet pan over medium-high heat. Add squid and fry 3 minutes. Drain oil from pan. Reduce heat to low and add butter. In a medium-size bowl, beat eggs with salt and pepper until just mixed. Pour into pan and cook 1 minute. Transfer to oven and bake 10 minutes. Do not fold this omelet. Serves 4.

—— Tan Chaio (Half Moon) Omelets ——

4 eggs
Salt and pepper

Filling:
2 tablespoons butter
4 oz. peeled and deveined cooked shrimp,
 finely chopped
1 tablespoon soy sauce
1 tablespoon dry sherry
1 teaspoon sugar
1/2 teaspoon salt

Vegetable oil
8 oz. chopped cooked spinach or peas
2/3 cup chicken broth, heated

In a medium-size bowl, beat eggs with salt and pepper until just mixed; set aside. *For filling:* Melt butter in a small skillet over low heat. Add shrimp, soy sauce, sherry, sugar and salt and toss 3 minutes. Set a small (4-inch, if available) omelet pan over low heat and brush with a little oil. Pour in 1 tablespoon egg. Quickly spoon 2 teaspoons filling on one side of egg; fold over and press edges gently to seal. Turn omelet with a metal spatula and cook 20 seconds longer. Remove and set aside. Continue until eggs and filling are used.

Place a large skillet over low heat and oil lightly. Add spinach or peas. Arrange omelets in a single layer over vegetables. Pour in hot broth, cover and simmer 5 minutes. Garnish with cooked, peeled prawns, if desired. Serves 4.

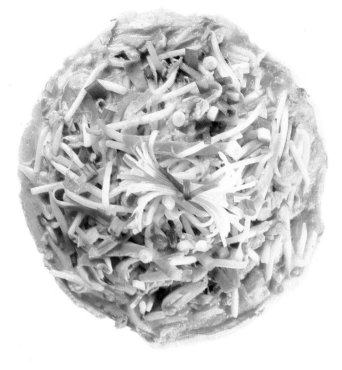

Egg Foo Yung

4 eggs
1 tablespoon soy sauce
1 tablespoon vegetable oil
2 oz. cooked ham, shredded
3 oz. bean sprouts
4 green onions, finely chopped

Preheat broiler. In a small bowl, beat eggs
with soy sauce until just mixed. Set 7-
inch omelet pan over low heat to become
thoroughly hot. Add oil. When hot, stir in
ham, bean sprouts and onion. Cook, stirring constantly, 2 minutes.

Pour in eggs and stir with a fork until
mixture has just set. Broil until golden-
brown, about 1 minute. Garnish with
green onions, if desired. Serves 2.

—— Caviar-Topped Miniature Omelets ——

6 eggs
Salt and pepper
2 tablespoons butter
2 oz. caviar
2/3 cup sour cream
Coriander sprigs

In a medium-size bowl, beat eggs with salt and pepper until just mixed. Heat a little butter in omelet pan over low heat. Add 2 tablespoons egg and cook until just set. Lift onto a baking sheet and keep warm. Repeat until all eggs are used.

Spoon a little caviar over each omelet. Top with sour cream. Fold over, garnish with coriander sprigs and serve immediately. If preferred, the omelets may be left to cool before filling and serving. Serves 4.

Savory Walnut Omelet

6 eggs
3/4 cup finely chopped walnuts
1/3 cup currants or raisins
1/4 cup fresh white bread crumbs
2 tablespoons chopped fresh chives
1/4 teaspoon turmeric
Salt and pepper
2 tablespoons butter
Chopped walnuts and mint sprigs

In a medium-size bowl, beat eggs until just mixed. Fold in walnuts, currants, bread crumbs, chives, turmeric, salt and pepper.

Preheat broiler. Melt butter in an 8-inch omelet pan over low heat. Pour in egg mixture and cook until set. Broil until top is golden-brown, about 1 minute. Cut into quarters. Garnish with chopped walnuts and mint sprigs. Serves 4.

Italian Country Frittata

4 tablespoons vegetable oil
1 medium-size zucchini, diced
1 celery stalk, diced
2 medium-size tomatoes, peeled, seeded
  and chopped
Salt and pepper
4 eggs
2 tablespoons grated Parmesan cheese
1 teaspoon chopped fresh basil
Extra Parmesan cheese for sprinkling
Mint sprigs

Heat 2 tablespoons oil in a large skillet over low heat. Add zucchini and celery and cook gently 5 minutes. Add tomatoes, salt and pepper and simmer, stirring occasionally, for 15 minutes.

In a small bowl, beat eggs with cheese and basil. Add remaining oil to pan and heat 1 minute. Pour in egg mixture and cook 4 minutes. Carefully flip mixture and continue cooking second side 4 minutes. Cut into quarters and sprinkle with Parmesan. Garnish with mint sprigs and serve immediately. Serves 4.

French Picnic Omelet

3 eggs
3 tablespoons cold water
Salt and pepper
4 tablespoons butter
1 small baguette French bread
8 slices salami
3 medium-size tomatoes, sliced
Watercress sprigs

In a small bowl, beat eggs with water, salt and pepper until just mixed. Set 7-inch omelet pan over low heat to become thoroughly hot. Add 2 tablespoons butter. Increase heat slightly and add eggs. Using a fork or spatula, draw mixture from sides to middle of pan, allowing uncooked egg to run underneath and set quickly. Repeat until egg mixture is lightly cooked.

Split bread in half lengthwise; spread surface lightly with remaining butter and set on a plate. Using a metal spatula, fold over 1/3 of omelet away from handle. Holding the handle with the palm of the hand on top, place the pan over 1/2 the bread. Shake omelet to edge of pan, tip completely over to make another fold and turn omelet onto bread. Top with salami, tomatoes and watercress. Top with remaining bread. To carry on a picnic, wrap in foil. Serves 4.

Spanish Omelet

1 tablespoon olive oil
2 medium-size tomatoes, peeled and
  quartered
1 small onion, finely chopped
1 small green pepper, finely chopped
1 thick slice cooked ham, diced
1 medium-size potato, cooked, diced
1 garlic clove, crushed
4 stuffed green olives, sliced
4 eggs
Salt and pepper

Heat oil in a large skillet over low heat.
Add tomatoes, onion, green pepper,
ham, potato and garlic. Cook, stirring
often, until vegetables are tender, 7 to 8
minutes. Stir in olives.

Preheat broiler. In a small bowl, beat eggs
with salt and pepper until just mixed.
Pour over vegetables and cook 3 minutes.
Broil until top is golden-brown, about 1
minute. Cut omelet in half and slide each
half onto a hot serving plate. Serves 2.

Omelet Con Carne

1 tablespoon vegetable oil
1/2 lb. ground beef
1 (14-oz.) can tomatoes
1 small green pepper, cut in strips
1/2 teaspoon Tabasco sauce
1/2 teaspoon salt
6 eggs, separated
3 tablespoons tomato juice
Salt and pepper
2 tablespoons butter
Strips of green pepper and tortilla chips

Heat oil in a medium-size skillet over low heat. Add ground beef and stir until lightly browned. Add undrained tomatoes, green pepper and Tabasco sauce. Simmer, stirring often, 20 minutes. Season with salt. Keep warm.

Preheat broiler. In a medium-size bowl, beat egg yolks until thick and pale. Fold in tomato juice, salt and pepper. In another bowl, beat egg whites until stiff. Fold into egg yolks. Melt butter in an 8-inch omelet pan. Pour in egg mixture and cook until puffy and just set. Broil until top is golden, about 1 minute. Lift onto serving plate and top with meat sauce. Garnish with green pepper strips and tortilla chips. Serves 2 to 3.

Pipérade

1/4 cup butter
1 large onion, finely sliced
2 green peppers, cut into strips
1 garlic clove, crushed
1 lb. tomatoes, peeled and chopped
Salt and pepper
1/4 lb. sliced bacon
6 eggs
Parsley sprig

Melt butter in a large skillet over low heat. Add onion and cook 5 minutes. Add green pepper and garlic and cook 5 minutes. Add tomatoes, salt and pepper. Cover and cook 20 minutes.

Meanwhile, grill or fry bacon; keep hot. In a medium-size bowl, beat eggs thoroughly. Add to tomato mixture and, using a fork, lift eggs constantly until just set. Spoon onto a warm flat serving dish and cover with bacon. Garnish with parsley sprig. Serves 4.

Italian Pizza Omelet

1 tablespoon vegetable oil
1 small onion, finely chopped
1 (7-oz.) can tomatoes
Pinch of marjoram
Salt and pepper

2 Basic Omelets (page 76)

2 oz. button mushrooms, thinly sliced
1 medium-size tomato, sliced
1 oz. Mozzarella cheese, thinly sliced
4 thin slices salami, halved
Marjoram sprigs and capers

Prepare topping before making omelets. Heat oil in a small saucepan over low heat. Add onion and cook 3 minutes. Add undrained tomatoes, marjoram, salt and pepper. Simmer uncovered until reduced by half, about 10 minutes.

Preheat broiler. Make omelets. When 2/3 cooked, spoon half the tomato mixture over each one. Top each with half the mushrooms, tomato and cheese. Broil until cheese is melted and top of egg is set, about 1 minute. Roll salami halves into cones and place 4 on each omelet. Garnish with marjoram and capers. Serve immediately. Serves 2.

INDEX